San Diego's

Finest Athletes
Five Exceptional Lives

San Diego's
Finest Athletes
Five Exceptional Lives

Foreword by Nick Canepa

Joey Seymour

SUNBELT PUBLICATIONS

San Diego, California
www.sunbeltbooks.com

San Diego's Finest Athletes: Five Exceptional Lives
Sunbelt Publications, Inc

Copyright © 2009 by the author
All rights reserved. First edition 2009

Edited by Iris Engstrand
Cover and book design by Designs by Allen Wynar

Sunbelt Publications, Inc.
P.O. Box 191126
San Diego, CA 92159-1126
(619) 258-4911, fax: (619) 258-4916
www.sunbeltbooks.com

13 12 11 10 09   5 4 3 2 1

Library of Congress Cataloging-in-Publication Data

Seymour, Joey.
  San Diego's finest athletes : five exceptional lives / by Joey Seymour.
p. cm.
  Includes bibliographical references.
  ISBN 978-0-916251-99-4
  1. Athletes--United States--Biography. 2. Woman athletes--United States--Biography. 3. Connolly, Maureen, 1934-1969. 4. Powell, Charlie. 5. Louganis, Greg, 1960- 6. Chin, Tiffany, 1967- 7. Gonzales, Adrian. I. Title.
  GV697.A1S46 2009
  796.0922--dc22
  [B]
                        2009029595

For Shay

Acknowledgements

I would greatly like to thank the following people, without whom this process would have been significantly more difficult and in many cases, impossible. In an effort to remain fair, since everyone's participation was vital, I have listed my acknowledgements in alphabetical order.

Terry Batt: There is no way I could have felt confident about turning in my chapters without your editorial assistance and emotional support.

Patrick Down: Thank you for all the research assistance at the San Diego Hall of Champions.

Dr. Iris Engstrand: Thank you for serving as my mentor and for your constant reassurances in my abilities to complete this.

Dr. Colin Fisher: Your support early on in this process gave me the confidence to see it through and I am very grateful.

Adrian Gonzalez: I hope you enjoy the chapter on your accomplishments as much I enjoyed researching and writing about them. Thank you for the interview. It added much more depth to the chapter. I wish you and your wife Betsy all the best with your foundation. Go, Padres!

Dr. Michael Gonzalez: Thank you for welcoming me into this program with open arms and challenging me in your classroom.

Billie Jean King: Your willingness to consistently spare a few minutes for me and my projects is incredible and always cherished.

Melinda King: I can't imagine having gone through this process without you. You are the greatest writing partner in the world. I wish you luck with your thesis and know that it will be just as amazing as you are.

Greg Louganis: Your accomplishments in sport are secondary to your kindness and good nature. Thank you so much for allowing me to interview you. There is no chapter in this project of which I am more proud. You are an inspiration and I thank you again from the bottom of my heart.

Dr. Molly McClain: I appreciate you serving as my second reader. Your input and suggestions were warmly welcomed.

Tip Nunn: Thank you once again for assisting me in my interview with Ms. King.

David Ochoa: There is not another person on this list that had more to do with the creation of this project. You are my guiding light and the reason for attempting this journey in the first place. Your companionship, loyalty, and faith in me allowed me to forge on during the most difficult moments of this process. There is nothing I can write that will truly express my appreciation for you. All I can say is that this is as much your project as it is mine.

Jennifer Redmond and the staff at Sunbelt Publications: Thank you for taking a chance on me and this book. It is a honor to be a member of the Sunbelt family.

Todd Tobias: Your assistance with my research at the San Diego Hall of Champions was the backbone of this project. There is no way that I would have been able to write this without your help and the access you gave me to your files. I also want to thank you for allowing me to interview you.

Nhu Tran: Thank you for setting up the interview with Adrian Gonzalez. Your professionalism and kindness was very much appreciated.

Alan Valantine: You are a great friend and your willingness to always step up and help me is remarkable. Thank you for everything you did to assist in setting up the interview with Adrian Gonzalez, but more importantly, thank you for always having my back.

Allen Wynar: Your incredible design work has turned my dream into reality. Thank you for your patience, talent and expertise.

Table of Contents

Preface   1

Foreword   5

Introduction   11

I   San Diego's Sweetheart: Maureen Connolly   15

II   A Look at the Professional Sporting Careers of   49
     Chillin' Charlie Powell

III Greg Louganis: San Diego's Dominant Diver   79

IV   Tiffany Chin: San Diego's Ice Princess   115

V   Adrian Gonzalez: From Little League in Tijuana to   145
     First Base at Petco Park

VI   A Legacy of Champions   169

     Afterword   185

     Bibliography   189

Preface

The creation of this book occurred in an incredibly unlikely manner. I was serving in my first season as the ticket sales manager for the Newport Beach Breakers, a professional tennis team in Orange County, California, when my boss called and told me to go pick up Billie Jean King from her hotel. At first I thought he was joking. Apparently, the driver who had been arranged for her was not available, and so the responsibility fell on me. I quickly cleaned out the fast food bags from the back seat of my dirty Hyundai and raced to the hotel. I arrived and was told that she would be waiting outside for me. I was very nervous; it's not every day that you are asked to drive an icon of American sport around. I finally spotted her. She was talking on her cell phone. I opened the passenger door and she got in. She continued to talk on her cell phone as we drove. It did not matter to me. I was just shocked and delighted to have her in the car with me. She finished her conversation, turned to me and introduced herself. She then proceeded to ask me questions about myself. I stumbled a bit, thinking, "why would she have any interest in me?" But I soon found myself telling her about my previous jobs in the sports industry and my desire to go back to school, get my master's degree in history and write books about historical moments and athletes in sports.

With all the enthusiasm and emotion that she displayed

while competing, she told me to go for it. She explained that
she too had a love of history and that she believed I could do it.
Before the end of my first season with the Breakers, I had been
accepted into the University of San Diego's history department,
and two years later I handed Billie Jean her copy of my master's
thesis, which has since become this book. It still amazes me that
my encounter with Billie Jean King took place and that Sunbelt
Publications agreed to publish this project. I thank them both and
am honored that you are reading this. I truly hope that you will
enjoy the stories of the lives and careers of the athletes within.

Another remarkable moment in the development of this
book was the inclusion of the foreword by Nick Canepa. Nick is
not only one of the most notable sports writers in the country,
but he has been someone whom I have respected and admired
for many years. His writing style is unique and captivating.
Nick has been documenting San Diego sports moments since
he began with the *San Diego Union-Tribune* in 1974. His career,
knowledge of San Diego sports and passion for writing are all
elements that I hope to one day achieve myself. I thank Nick for
assisting me and hope you enjoy his addition to this book.

San Diego sports fans have suffered a lot of heartache
over the years. In fact, none of their professional sports teams
has ever won a championship. They've come close, but have
never brought home a title to San Diego. Yet, some of the most
incredible athletes have come from San Diego, specifically those
discussed in this book. Researching their lives and retelling their
stories was a fascinating experience for me, during the process of
writing my thesis. However, I wanted to share their stories with

the San Diego sports fans with the goal being, that they might remember or learn for the first time just how extraordinary these athletes from their own backyard were/are. That is why I am so proud to have had the opportunity to publish this book. Even though San Diegans may not have a World Series to brag about or a Super Bowl title (yet), the accomplishments of these athletes, not only their athletic achievements, but the racial and sexual barriers that they overcame so that future generations of minority athletes would not have to face the same scrutiny and struggles, is something of which all San Diegans should be proud. I thank both Greg Louganis and Adrian Gonzalez for their contributions to this book and hope that Tiffany Chin, Charlie Powell and the family of Maureen Connolly all enjoy the chapters dedicated to them.

A final note: no one believed more in me or in the completion of this book than Dr. Iris Engstrand at the University of San Diego. With an incredible resume of historical works herself, she took me under her guidance and saw this project through from the first outline to the final approval of the cover art work. There are no other words that I can use to thank her for all that she has done.

I hope you enjoy reading about these five exceptional minority athletes from San Diego, as they are truly some of the finest.

Joey Seymour
July 4, 2009

Foreword by Nick Canepa

Both of my parents were born in San Diego, making me a second generation San Diegan, my three sons third, my five grandchildren fourth. All live within a few miles of my home. What this means is that we are rarities, especially the grandkids. You know what people like to say: San Diego is a city largely made up of people from someplace else.

Given that, this means there are a whole lot of transplants who really aren't totally up on the great San Diego athletes I've been writing about for nearly four decades on the sports staff of the *San Diego Union-Tribune*. But we have had our share – more than our share. As an example, no other U.S. city can claim four Heisman Trophy winners – Marcus Allen, Rashan Salaam, Ricky Williams and Reggie Bush. San Diego can. No other city can claim to be the birthplace of the last major league hitter to bat .400. Ted Williams was a San Diegan, born and raised.

And there are so many more, such as golfers Mickey Wright, Phil Mickelson, Billy Casper, Gene Littler, Craig Stadler and Scott Simpson, tennis greats Mo Connelly and Michael Chang, track stars Gail Devers and Arnie Robinson, basketball's Bill Walton and Ann Meyers-Drysdale, boxing's Archie Moore, figure skating's Tiffany Chin, football's Junior Seau, Terrell Davis, Brick Muller and Willie Buchanon,

Marcus Allen. Courtesy of the San Diego Hall of Champions.

baseball's Tony Gwynn and Adrian Gonzalez (to name two of a slew), diver Greg Louganis ... I'm leaving a whole lot of people out, but you get the picture. Walk through the Hall of Champions in Balboa Park and you'll get an even larger photograph of what this city has produced.

You can make an argument that San Diego produced the greatest hitter (Williams), female tennis player (Connolly), female golfer (Wright), and all-around football player (Allen). There are those who claim that, in one weight class (light heavyweight), no fighter was better or more dominant than Moore, the "Old Mongoose," whose staggering career knockout record of 145 may last until they start lining up on Judgment Day. Enjoy badminton? Dr. Dave Freeman is widely considered the greatest of them all. He never lost. That's right. Never.

It's apparent from Joey Seymour's fine book, "San Diego's Finest Athletes," that he has done exhaustive research on the subject. That he chose to single out Connolly, Charlie Powell, Greg Louganis, Chin and Gonzalez, makes a whole lot of sense. They were (are) terrific, and he couldn't write about every San Diego athlete unless he had about 20 years to study and write. There are great stories behind them all.

I am particularly attracted to the chapter on Charlie Powell, who may be the greatest all-around athlete the city has produced. He also attended my alma mater, San Diego High, where he was a four-sport athlete. When I attended San Diego back in the early 1960s, legend had it that one fateful day, Charlie won the shot put for the track team, changed uniforms and won the Cavers' baseball game with a home run.

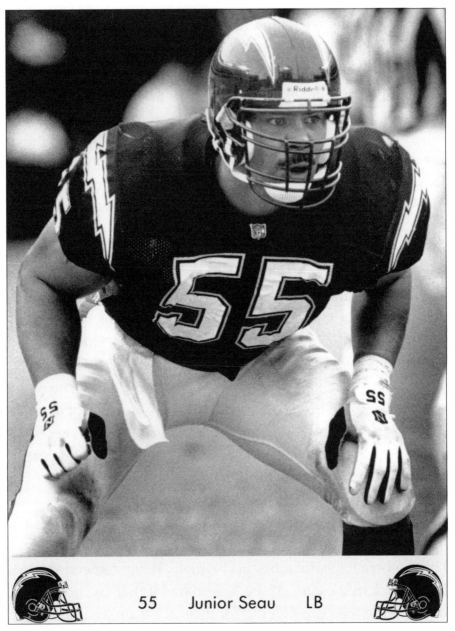

55   Junior Seau   LB

Junior Seau stares down an opponent. Courtesy of the San Diego Hall of Champions.

He played for the 49ers and he fought Muhammad Ali. Powell's brother, Art (also of SDHS) was a tremendous wide receiver, named to the all-time AFL team.

These are all great stories, and all together they make for fascinating reading. I'm sure many people new to the area will be surprised to see some of these names, not knowing he or she was from San Diego. But they were and are. If you've been around the city long enough you may not be surprised at all. But, then again, maybe you will be.

Introduction

There are moments within the realm of sport that have changed the world for members of oppressed groups of people. Then there are the athletes who created those moments. On April 15, 1947 before a crowd of 26,000 – 14,000 of which were African American – at Ebbets Field in Brooklyn, New York, Jackie Robinson took the field, breaking the color barrier that Major League Baseball had clung to tightly. Before leaving for the field, Jackie quipped to his wife Rachel, "Just in case you have trouble picking me out I'll be wearing number forty-two."[1]

On October 16, 1968, renowned sportswriter Dave Zirin detailed, "As the U.S. flag began rising up the flagpole and the anthem played, [Tommie] Smith and [John] Carlos bowed their heads and raised their fists in a Black power salute, creating what is now a widely recognized image. But most people don't see that their medal stand included more than just the gloves. The two men also wore no shoes, to protest black poverty, and beads, to protest lynching."[2]

On September 20, 1973, Billie Jean King defeated Bobby Riggs in the famous "Battle of the Sexes" tennis match in Houston, Texas. According to Zirin, "King was far more than a symbol, or an athlete. She was a participant and activist in the women's movement for equal rights."[3] In 1981, both Billie Jean King and tennis rival Martina Navratilova came out publicly with the fact that they were lesbians. In 1999, Billy Bean, an outfielder for the Detroit Tigers, Los Angeles Dodgers, and San Diego Padres, was the first prominent male athlete on a team sport to announce that he was homosexual. These events have aided in bringing to the forefront the struggles faced by members of these minority groups. Even though struggles persist, the world of sports and these athletes have had a role in attempting to create a competitive atmosphere in which people are judged only on their abilities and not the color of their skin, gender, or sexual orientation.

San Diego has produced its own breed of athletes who have fought off stereotypes and segregation. And in doing so, they have paved the way for future athletes within minority groups to achieve success, much like the aforementioned athletes. The following chapters will examine the lives of five of these courageous competitors, their battles for legitimacy and equality, and their accomplishments both within and outside the sporting world. The first athlete was San Diego's sweetheart in the late 1940s and early 1950s, Maureen Connolly. The first female to incorporate a power game into the gentile sport of tennis — her dominance in the sport was fueled by an intense passion to win. She transformed the sport and opened the door for future female supremacy in a once male dominated sport.

Next is Charlie Powell, San Diego's first multi-sport athlete. Powell competed in professional baseball, football, and boxing – all during a time in which African Americans faced national bigotry and segregation. His participation on the field and in the ring provided proof that success in several sports was possible, especially inspiring to athletes across the board, particularly young African American men.

Greg Louganis, born of Pacific Islander descent, won a silver medal at the 1976 summer Olympics, two gold medals at the 1984 games, and two more in the summer of 1988, in the sport of diving.

He is also one of the first male athletes to publicly announce his homosexuality.

Fourth, the career of Tiffany Chin, the first Chinese American to win the United States National Figure Skating title and place fourth at an Olympic event. Tiffany opened the door for Asian American female domination in the sport, which continues today.

Finally, this book examines the early career of current San Diego Padres first baseman, Adrian Gonzalez. A product of both Chula Vista, California, and the town of Tijuana in Mexico, Gonzalez represents a positive role model for Mexican children on both sides of the border with aspirations of athletic success.

San Diego, a diverse and progressive community, has produced exceptional minority athletes. The goal of this book is to provide an in depth look at the lives and careers of five athletes by illustrating how their triumphs and victories over adversity opened the door for future generations of women and minority athletes. Also, to create an understanding that even though their stories may not be as famous as those of Jackie, Billie Jean, Martina, or Tommie and John, the fact remains that the accomplishments of Maureen, Charlie, Greg, Tiffany, and Adrian have played an important role in the quest for equality among all athletes and all human beings.

Endnotes

1. Jon Weisman, "A New Era Dawns: Tensions Mounted for Robinson on First Day," *www.si.com*, April 13, 2007.
2. Dave Zirin, *What's My Name, Fool: Sports and Resistance in the United States* (Chicago: Haymarket Books, 2005), 76.
3. Ibid., 205.

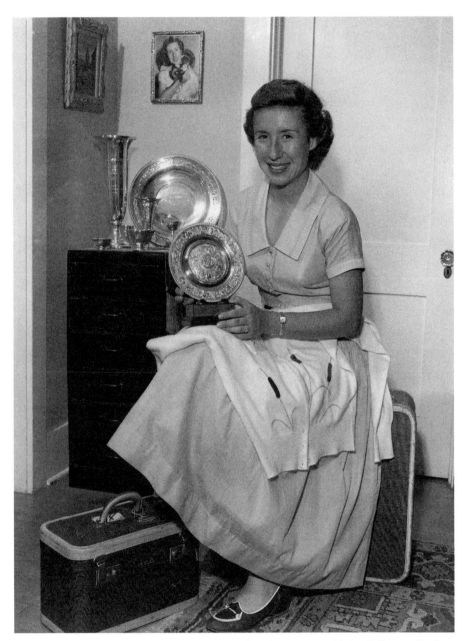

"Little Mo" arrives home victorious, 1954. ©SDHS, UT #84:3219-1, Union-Tribune collection.

Chapter I

San Diego's Sweetheart: Maureen Connolly

"I've got everything I want. Everything I've had, I got through tennis. It gave me a terribly exciting life. I met so many people in exalted positions. It opened so many doors and it's still opening them. I've had a wonderful life. If I should leave tomorrow, I've had the experience of 20 people."[1] – Maureen Connolly

Maureen Connolly was nationally recognized as a tennis star from San Diego in the 1950s. At age eleven, she was dubbed "Little Mo" by San Diego sports writer Nelson Fisher who claimed that her power forehand and backhand had the same firepower as the big guns of the *USS Missouri*.[2] The Associated Press named her female athlete of the year for three consecutive years (1952, 1953, and 1954), an honor she achieved by developing a particularly aggressive style of play. After her career came to a crashing halt on July 20, 1954, when she was thrown from her horse, "Little Mo" continued to pack a great deal into her life. She frequently told people, "I've lived ten lives." She was a tennis champion, newspaper reporter and author, wife, mother, restaurateur, sporting-goods spokeswoman, television and radio color commentator, philanthropist, and cancer victim, before dying at age thirty-four. The following article provides a retrospective look at the many lives of Maureen Connolly.

Early Life in San Diego and the Making of a Champion

On September 17, 1934, Jessamine and Martin Connolly awaited the birth of their first child at Mercy Hospital in San Diego. Martin, a lieutenant commander in the Navy, served as an athletic trainer. According to Arthur Voss, "Connolly had been a boxer and played baseball, football, and hockey, but not tennis."[3] Jessamine, who originally had hailed from Helena, Montana, danced and sang. Based on the baby's "lusty heartbeat," the obstetrician had assumed the newborn would be a boy. To everyone's surprise, a little girl—Maureen Catherine Connolly—was born. The new parents brought their baby girl home to their red brick bungalow on Idaho Street in the North Park district of San Diego.

The Connollys divorced when Maureen was only four. "My last memory of my father came when I was ill. He looked down at me, smiled and told me he would buy me a chocolate sundae, topped with nuts, when I recovered. We never heard from him, never knew where he might have gone."[4] Young Maureen was later told that he had died in an accident, a story that turned out to be false.

Maureen's mother, Jessamine, wanted her daughter to become the great musician and dancer that she herself never had the chance to become. According to Beverly Beyette, "the antithesis of the stage mother—a vacillating, indecisive woman, a frustrated would-be concert pianist who wound up playing for weddings and found vicarious pleasure in her daughter's triumphs."[5] Maureen attempted ballet, singing, and piano lessons but, "on her way to more tom-boy pursuits on the University Heights Playground," she stumbled across a tennis match being played by two local professionals, Gene Garrett and Arnie Saul. Enthralled by the sport, she soon learned that all she needed was "a racket in my hand to vanquish any little boy or girl in the neighborhood."[6]

Maureen served as a ball girl for the local tennis professional, Wilbur Folsom, who later began instructing the motivated ten year-old. "Folsom taught Maureen the rudiments – how to serve, how to hit the forehand and backhand drives, and how to execute proper footwork."[7] She had an inexpensive tennis racket that cost her mother $1.50. Unlike most top tennis competitors who trained at private tennis clubs, Maureen played on public courts owned and operated by the City of San Diego.

Her tournament career began in 1945 at the La Jolla Playground's annual tennis tournament. Maureen, playing in the thirteen-and-under category, made it to the finals but lost to an older girl named Ann Bissell. With this loss came the development of an angry, competitive streak rarely discussed in articles or remembrances written about "Little Mo." She wrote about it in *Forehand Drive*, an autobiography that she completed shortly after her career-ending accident: "I was no ordinary little girl, and tennis to me, even then, was much more than just a game. Defeat was unendurable; it could not be talked away by the sympathy of an understanding parent. It must be avenged!

Beating Ann Bissell became my single goal in life."[8]

Maureen did not love tennis but she hated losing. At ten years old, she feared that if she lost a match, no one would love her. Along with fear came anger. She would build up hatred for her opponent on the court in order to win. It is possible that both the abandonment of her father and the ambition of her mother helped to create this fierce attitude. According to one reporter, "She was like the other girls—small, slender, giggly, bands on the teeth, saying "sir" and "ma'am" when addressed by adults, but on the court, that was something else."[9]

Maureen's next tournament took place on her home court at University Heights Playground. Her first tournament victory was soured by the fact that Ann Bissell had not played. It was not until the 1946 Harper Ink Tournament that Maureen got a chance to face Bissell. The two girls competed in the final game of the tournament. The first set was a back-and-forth competition that Connolly eventually won 8-6. Seeking to embarrass her opponent, Little Mo bested Bissell in the next set, winning 6-2.[10]

Maureen won six more tournaments in 1946, competing in both the thirteen-and-under and the fifteen-and-under divisions. In 1947 she captured five more titles to find herself ranked number two among Southern California's girls under fifteen-years-old. Wilbur Folsom had tutored Maureen to the best of his ability. She practiced with boys, hitting just as hard and running just as fast as they did. But in order for Maureen's career to soar, she needed a new coach.

Eleanor "Teach" Tennant was known throughout Southern California as one of the best, if not *the* best, tennis instructors

A young Maureen Connolly prepares for a match. Courtesy of San Diego Hall of Champions.

Sixteen year-old Maureen Connolly practices at a public tennis court in San Diego, 1951. ©SDHS, UT #84:32877-1, Union-Tribune Collection.

in the region. She had coached champions such as Alice Marble, winner of five Grand Slam events between 1936 and 1940, and Bobby Riggs, best known for his Battle of the Sexes exhibition match versus Billie Jean King on September 20, 1973.[11] Born in San Francisco in 1895, Tennant played tennis at the famous Golden Gate Park courts. She later became the resident professional at the upscale Beverly Hills Hotel, teaching some of the biggest names in Hollywood at the time. Carole Lombard gave her the nickname, "Teach."[12]

Tennant met Maureen in 1948 and knew instantly that she had a potential star on her hands. Maureen, eager to learn, demonstrated her talent and dedication. Every weekend, she took the bus from San Diego to Beverly Hills to work with Tennant. However, she occasionally disagreed with, and disobeyed, her demanding teacher. One weekend, after she had received strict orders to practice, she was caught "rallying with actor Gilbert Roland, a friend who once took Maureen to the Tijuana bullfights and found himself with an almost inconsolable child on his hand when a horse was injured." Scolded and sent home to San Diego, Maureen wrote a letter of apology and was immediately forgiven.[13]

Teach became a second mother to Maureen, teaching her about life, dress, and most importantly, tennis. She worked diligently to improve Maureen's game. In 1948, Maureen won an impressive eighteen titles and was ranked as the number one girls singles player in Southern California. Tennant also encouraged the antagonism that Maureen felt for her opponents. She believed that tennis was not a game, but a fight. She would scout and analyze Maureen's opponents. "Eleanor Tennant contributed to my hate complex," she later wrote, "but there was fertile soil for the seed. She believed one should not make friends with opponents, one should remain aloof. I translated this into hating my foes. Miss Tennant, I am positive, had no idea a seed of hatred would flower in my breast with such a dark bloom."[14]

For Maureen, the year 1949 was stellar on the court but difficult at home. She won nine titles, became the youngest girl ever to win the junior national title at the age of fourteen, and played in her first women's tournament. However, her mother remarried a man whom Maureen disliked. Her new stepfather, Auguste Berste, was a local musician who did not appreciate tennis. According to a journalist, "Her mother's second husband opposed her obsession with the game, and the two clashed frequently."[15]

Sports writers loved Maureen, describing her as a "killer in pigtails." Her infectious smile and dazzling action pictures appeared in the local papers through 1950, when she won the national junior girls singles title and the doubles title with her partner and good friend Patsy Zellmer. She was ranked number nineteen among women players in the United States. The following year, 1951, her career took off.

The Championship Years

Maureen Connolly became a national celebrity in the summer of 1951 at Forest Hills, New York, home of the U.S. Open.[16] It was there that Eleanor Tennant concocted a devious

A focused Maureen moments before a match. Courtesy of the San Diego Hall of Champions.

Maureen, alongside her coach, Eleanor Tennant, receives one of her many trophies. Courtesy of the San Diego Hall of Champions.

ploy to further fuel Maureen's anger at her opponents. Maureen was facing Doris Hart, her idol and one of the great tennis legends, in the semi-finals. Tennant feared that Maureen did not have a chance, so she told her that she had overheard Doris call her "a spoiled brat" and say that she was "gunning for her." It was a lie, but it did the trick.[17]

It was an overcast New York day with a light drizzle. When

the match on Center Court began, Maureen looked nothing like a champion. She later wrote, "I never hated anyone more in my life! I turned on her like a tiger, but despite my fury–I tried to knock the cover off the ball–I managed to lose the first four games."[18] But Little Mo's rage and desire to destroy her opponent led to an epic comeback. Maureen won the next six games in a row, taking the set 6-4. In an exciting second set which saw Maureen take a 5-1 and seemingly insurmountable lead, Hart coming roaring back to make it 5-4. Still, this was Little Mo's moment and no one was going to stop her. She won the next game and the match.

Sixteen-year-old Maureen made it to the finals of the U.S. Open where she faced Shirley Fry, Hart's best friend on the tour and a formidable opponent in her own right. Shirley wanted to avenge the loss of her friend and take the title. Connolly wanted it just a bit more. . .and so did Tennant. The opening two sets went smoothly. In the first set, Maureen dominated Shirley 6-3. Shirley returned to defeat Maureen 6-1. During the ten-minute break between sets, Tennant looked sternly into Maureen's eyes. "You will have to control your hitting. To do that you'll have to move faster and you'll have to do it even if it kills you to win this set. Forget you're tired. You're in the big leagues now. You can't submit to fatigue. Concentrate on your game…you must win!"[19] And win she did. Maureen battled Fry and, at match point, rejoiced as Fry's backhand return sailed out.

Maureen was now the youngest U.S. Open Champion in history. Associated Press voted her Woman Athlete of the Year and she was ranked as the number one women's tennis player in the United States.[20] On September 17, 1951, *Time Magazine* noted that even though "women's tennis had been in the doldrums since 1941, when Alice Marble left the scene, a Forest Hills gallery last week stood up and cheered with new hope for a sturdy, rosy-cheeked girl who will not turn 17 until next week. Maureen Connolly clearly was a good notch above her tournament competition."[21]

The year 1952 brought joy as well as sadness as "Little Mo" became an international star. She defeated archrival Doris Hart for her second consecutive U.S. Open title before venturing to London to play in the Wimbledon Championships. However, before she took her first step on the famous grass courts at the All England Lawn Tennis Club, she parted ways with Tennant over a medical diagnosis. After feeling a slight pain in her shoulder, Maureen visited a local trainer who had said she had a bit of bursitis and that a simple ointment would help. Tennant wanted another opinion. The two visited a chiropractor who claimed that Maureen had a torn muscle. Teach, not wanting her star pupil to risk further damage, told the press that Maureen would default the tournament. Maureen disagreed and, in an unprecedented move, called a press conference and told journalists, "Miss Tennant no longer represents my views."[22] Her daughter, Cindy Brinker Simmons, later wrote that this was a "first" in Wimbledon history: "No player had ever done this before. The press adored Mom, so when 'Little Mo' spoke, everybody came running."[23]

She played brilliantly, and disposed of her early round opponents only to find herself pitted against three-time

"Little Mo" in action. Courtesy of the San Diego Hall of Champions.

Wimbledon champion, Louise Brough. She wrote, "I was nervous against Louise. I had beaten her at La Jolla, but before coming to Wimbledon she had trimmed me 5-8, 6-2, and 6-2,

Maureen Connolly receives a ticker tape parade down Broadway after winning Wimbledon, 1952. Courtesy of the San Diego Hall of Champions.

at the Southern California Tennis Championships in Los Angeles."[24] Little Mo had nothing to be nervous about for, after a spirited effort in the first set, Brough's nerves got the best of her. Connolly became the world's champion with a 7-5, 6-3 victory. However, by dismissing Tennant, she had lost an important and valuable figure in her life. She wrote, "Our quarrel on the eve of Wimbledon left me emotionally torn. It was difficult for a young girl to draw charity's veil over bitterness, to rationalize, compensate and reconcile."[25] Maureen apologized to Teach in her autobiography but, according to Brinker, "they never spoke again. Still all her life, Mom regretted the incident and its outcome."[26]

Maureen met her next coach, Henry "Harry" Hopman, after her victory at Wimbledon. Captain-coach of twenty-two Australian Davis Cup teams between 1939 and 1967, he would guide her through the next two years of her career. He and his wife helped her to change her attitude toward her opponents. Nell Hopman sat her down before an exhibition match in Australia and explained that her "tennis would not suffer if she cast off hate and fear." Maureen disagreed since "this would be throwing away my two most potent weapons."[27] However, when matched against friend Julie Sampson, she found that she could no longer hate her opponent across the net. Instead, she focused only on her instincts and reflexes. For the first time in her career, Maureen Connolly enjoyed herself while competing on the tennis court.

Maureen's success in 1952 was impressive. She won two of the four major tournaments, Wimbledon and the U.S. Open, and the Associated Press once again voted her woman athlete of the year.[28]

San Diego, proud of its native daughter, welcomed her home with a parade, an honor, and a gift. An estimated fifteen thousand people lined Broadway in downtown San Diego to see the tennis star. Maureen, wearing a white dress, rode in the back of a white convertible. Mayor John D. Butler declared September 9, 1952 to be "Maureen Connolly Day" in San Diego. Supporters organized a Maureen Connolly Appreciation Fund with five hundred and sixty four contributors. She received a horse as a token of appreciation for "what she had done for the town, for the way she has made it a big name in the world."[29] Maureen selected a majestic Tennessee walking horse named Colonel Merryboy.

In 1953, Maureen became engaged to Norman Brinker who, at that time, served in the U.S. Navy. According to one journalist, "The courtship was marked by partings and reunions—when he came home from the Western Pacific during the Korean War, when she came back from the European tournament circuit. There was a religious conflict; she was Roman Catholic, he a Methodist. But when she returned, triumphant, from her 1953 victory at Wimbledon, they drove to Balboa Park one night and he slipped a diamond ring on her finger."[30] The couple decided to make a formal announcement after she returned from Europe.

Maureen's games at the Australian Championship, where she defeated Julie Sampson 6-3, 6-2, and French Open revealed her to be an accomplished player and a mature woman. In

Connelly poses prior to a match. Courtesy of the San Diego Hall of Champions.

Paris, she faced Doris Hart, her former foe and now friend, whom she defeated 6-2, 6-4. She then traveled to London to defend the Wimbledon title. On January 6, 1953, she again played Hart in the finals match. The two competed in what the press described as an emotional war. Doris was determined not to allow Maureen to defeat her this time. Maureen recalled that they both "went for broke." She took the first set 8-6 with only one point, set point, separating their point total. The second set would be the same. Maureen won the set 7-5, once again with only one point, championship point, being the difference. As the two champions walked off the court, Doris leaned over to Maureen and said, "this is the first time in my life I have lost a match and still felt as though I had won it."[31]

The Connolly-Hart match was described as one of the greatest women's finals ever played at Wimbledon. Neville Deed writing for *The Racquet*, stated: "The all-American final will go down in history as one of the best women's matches ever played anywhere. In my experience, which goes back to the 1910 Wimbledon, I do not remember there to have been a better one. It was the perfect pattern of how the game should be played."[32] English footballer David Jack told the *Empire News*: "It was a privilege to be a spectator…it must have been one of the greatest women's matches ever played."[33] Unfortunately, Maureen's joy did not last long. She received a telephone call from her good friend, *San Diego Union* sportswriter Nelson Fisher, who informed her that her fiancé Norman Brinker was being shipped-out to Korea. She broke down and wept.

Maureen returned to San Diego to prepare for the U.S.

Open. She found, to her surprise that Norman had not yet shipped out. They had only a few hours together but their time together gave her renewed confidence. At the U.S. Open, Maureen faced a newcomer on the circuit, Althea Gibson, the first African American woman to play at the tournament. Maureen wrote, "It is my conviction that any championship tournament would become a travesty if a great player were barred for reasons of color or race. I liked Althea and our relationship had been friendly."[34] In the final, Maureen faced a familiar rival, Doris Hart, to capture the title 6-2, 6-4. She became the first woman to win the Calendar Year Grand Slam of Tennis after taking the title at the Australian Championships, French Open, Wimbledon, and the U.S. Open and the only one to do it without losing a single set.[35] She captured fourteen titles in 1953 while still just eighteen-years-old.

On learning that the Associated Press, once again, voted her Woman Athlete of the Year, Maureen said, "I am very, very grateful to those who voted for me and I shall try to deserve it by playing my best in 1954."[36] The year started out well. She won all ten tournaments in which she played, including the 1954 Wimbledon Championship defeating Louise Brough 6-2, 7-5. It was her third consecutive Wimbledon title. Jack Murphy, writing for the *San Diego Union,* noted: "Little Mo gave another fine exhibition of controlled tennis, almost mechanical in its efficiency, to overcome her 31-year old opponent."[37] She was ranked number one in the world and nothing would bring her down…nothing except a horse and a cement truck driver.

The Accident

Sports writer Nelson Fisher reported on July 21, 1954:

> Little Mo, a columnist for the *San Diego Union*,
> had returned home Monday morning after winning
> her second National Clay Court title and her third
> Wimbledon crown. Almost the first thing she did was to
> ride her horse, Colonel Merryboy, which was given to her
> two years ago after she won her first Wimbledon title. In
> an interview before she went into surgery, Little Mo said:
> 'We were riding along the road (on Friars Road in Mission
> Valley). We stopped our horses as the truck approached.
> Colonel Merryboy shied and whirled into the truck. My
> leg was caught between my horse and the truck.[38]

Maureen broke her fibula and tore some muscles in the
accident, which took place at 1:30 p.m. on July 20. A nurse,
Kathryn Walker, who happened to be on her way to work,
watched the scene unfold and rushed to aid the fallen tennis
star. Maureen was taken to Mercy Hospital and was operated on
by Dr. Bruce Kimball. After the surgery, Kimball told reporters
that Maureen would not be able to play for a month. However,
he did not feel the injury would cost her career.[39]

Among all the well-wishers who visited the hospital was
her father. She recalled, "A well-set-up man, with short grey
hair, wearing a neat brown suit, came into my room. We looked
at each other for a moment, then I was in my father's arms.

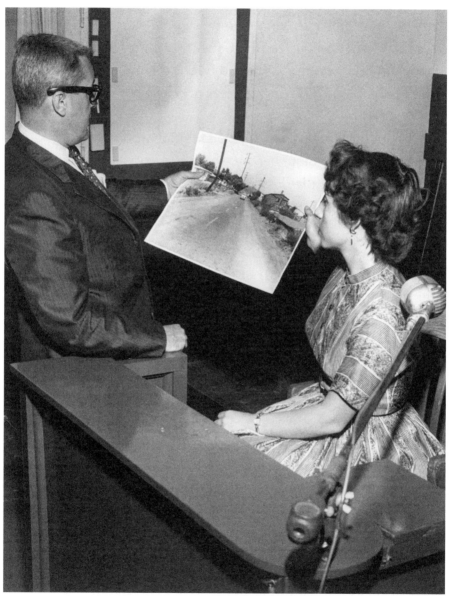

Connolly testifies during her trial vs. the Cement Mixing company whose truck driver caused her career-ending accident. Pictured with Maureen is her attorney, Melvin H. Belli. Courtesy of the San Diego Hall of Champions.

Only because of my accident had he stepped across the chasm
of years. It was a joyous reunion, the beginning of a new and
wonderful relationship."[40] She did not hear from her fiancé,
Norman Brinker, who was overseas and had not yet learned of
the accident.

Although Maureen had all the ambition and willpower
necessary to rehabilitate herself, she could not overcome her
injuries. She took ballet lessons to help regain her strength
and agility. She also returned to the tennis court in order to
preserve her powerful back and forehand, though she avoided
running. She thought that she might return to competition until,
in an exhibition match with Les Stoefen in January 1955, she
attempted to reach a tricky drop shot and felt shooting pains
through her right leg. She knew the result. Soon afterward, she
announced with sadness that her career was over. Billie Jean
King noted, "It was sad she had to retire so early because we
don't know how many more major titles she could have won. It
would have been great to see her compete against Tracy Austin
or Chris Evert, or even at the other end of the spectrum against
Martina Navratilova."[41] Instead, she found a new life as a wife,
mother, sportswriter, and entrepreneur.

Life After Tennis

Maureen's fiancé, Norman Brinker, also suffered a serious
accident while horseback riding. After his discharge from the
service, he had traveled to Hungary with the United States
Modern Pentathlon team. While he had been chosen for his

horsemanship, he also proved to be a strong runner, swimmer, shooter, and fencer. During the competition, Norman was on his horse preparing for the first jump. "I was low, but as we approached the jump, my horse flattened out a bit, and when he leaped he miscalculated, making his jump too soon. He hit the top of the logs, fell and slid...as we slid along the horse's head hit my shoulder and shattered it."[42] Norman, then twenty-three years old, was laid up in bed, and became a minor celebrity in Hungary.

When Maureen heard the news of Norman's accident while at her desk at the *San Diego Union*, she wrote to him at once and professed her love. When he returned home, they renewed their faltering romance and married on June 11, 1955. Teddy Tinling, who had created most of her tennis outfits, designed her wedding gown. Maureen recalled, "The bishop deviated from the usual marriage ceremony by giving a short talk about Norman and me as an ideal young couple – both accomplished athletes, each a credit to the world of sport. It was not planned; it flowed from his heart."[43] Their honeymoon took them to Europe where Maureen was beginning her career as a reporter. She wrote about the 1955 Wimbledon championship for the *London Daily Mail*. She felt strange not to be playing, but she described herself as happy with her new life.

Maureen's accident did not defeat her. She believed that her post-tennis career and family life gave her the satisfaction of a life lived by "ten people." Soon after her marriage, Little Mo became "Little Mom" with two daughters, Cindy and Brenda. She also wrote sports columns and served on the board of

Wilson Sporting Goods Company. Her husband, meanwhile, operated several successful "Jack-in-the-Box" restaurants.[44]

Although her injuries did not allow her to play competitive tennis, she was able to play in one-set exhibition matches. Crowds turned out to get a glimpse of Little Mo. According to one writer, "Even after her retirement, when hobbled by injury, Maureen fascinated San Diego's Community Concourse. She made believers out of persons to whom she was only a legend. In the concourse, she routed Nancy Kiner, 8-2, on a slick wood surface, which was expected to favor Nancy, who had won three indoor titles on that type of footing years previously. Nancy was more impressed than anybody. 'Once you've got it, you never lose it,' Nancy gasped."[45]

Maureen also served as a radio and television commentator. Billie Jean King remembered her "as being such a winner" and "also very smart. I liked the fact that she came from a public park background. As a player she was extremely tenacious and a great striker of the ball. Years later I learned that the first year I won Wimbledon in singles (1966) she was the commentator for BBC. That was a great moment for me when I heard her voice on tape as we were going through video for the HBO documentary *Portrait of a Pioneer*."[46]

In 1958, Maureen won a settlement against the company that operated the cement-mixer truck, which prematurely ended her career. The case went through several appeals before the California Supreme Court finally awarded Maureen $110,734, the largest personal injury award ever granted, up to that time, in San Diego. Unfortunately, the result was a great

The Brinker family visited Sea World prior to one of Maureen's final exhibition matches, 1968. Pictured are Maureen Connolly-Brinker, Norman Brinker, Cindy Brinker, and Brenda Brinker. ©SDHS, UT #85:H689-1, Union-Tribune Collection.

deal of negative publicity for Maureen. The citizens who had given her the horse now attacked her for riding it. She wrote, "Many people could not understand why I should have won an award in court. I had not been crippled. On the surface, at least, I appeared quite normal. 'What was she doing on a horse?' was the comment of some."[47] She was devastated by the popular reaction, particularly since she had done so much to promote the image of the city.

Soon afterward, the Brinker family moved to Dallas, Texas, where Maureen turned her attention to education. She became an undergraduate at Southern Methodist University in 1964. Her husband recalled, "Maureen was not able to get a college degree because of her tennis career. So when she finally went, she was a student *par excellence*. She managed to complete about two years worth of courses at SMU, going mainly at night, before her health deteriorated too far. She attacked college with the same concentration she displayed on the tennis courts."[48]

She also helped her husband with his new business, Brinks Coffee Shop in Dallas. A journalist noted, "Now Maureen is lending a helping hand in the opening of a fancy coffee shop, the family's first venture into business for themselves and one they hope to make the first of a chain of moderate priced restaurants in and out of Dallas."[49] Later, Norman created the Steak & Ale Restaurant and Bennigan's Grill & Tavern, both of which became successful chains. During this time, Maureen gave tennis lessons to youngsters. She enjoyed teaching and worked with her daughter, Cindy, who would later become a ranked collegiate player.

In 1968, she co-founded the Maureen Connolly Brinker Tennis Foundation to provide funds for tennis clinics and to aid juniors who could not afford to compete nationally. Her good friend, Nancy Jeffett, became her partner in this venture and continues to serve as co-founder and chairman emeritus.[50] Every year, the foundation sponsors six junior tournaments and three tournaments for women. Billie Jean King said of the foundation, "Her legacy continues through the Maureen Connolly Brinker Foundation. Nancy Jeffett and everyone at the foundation have done a great job to ensure that girls have an opportunity to compete in our sport at the highest levels. The foundation is definitely one of a kind and a great reflection on Maureen's contribution to tennis."[51]

Unfortunately, Little Mo did not live to see her foundation thrive. On May 21, 1969, Maureen Connolly lost her battle with cancer. She was thirty-four years old. At her funeral service, Reverend Robert N. Watkin, Jr. remarked, "It takes courage to come back from an 0-5 set on the tennis courts. It takes courage to come back from a terrible horseback riding accident to lead a full life. And it takes courage to face almost certain death with her chin held high. She had the courage."[52] A year before she died, knowing that her cancer was inoperable, she went to the bedside of her childhood friend and former doubles partner, Patsy Zellmer, who also was dying of cancer. According to one author, "She had the guts to go and try to cheer her up. That was the only experience that unnerved her a little."[53]

Maureen's tombstone reads, "Wife, Mother, Champion," but she was much more than that. She was a complicated and hurt girl who used her inner rage to propel her to greatness in the tennis world; a mature champion who was able to let go of the pain, anger, hatred, and fear; a wife who helped her husband to create successful businesses; a mother who nurtured and educated her young daughters; a businesswoman; a respected television and radio personality; an author who published two books and wrote numerous articles, and the co-founder of a foundation that continues to help young players today. This was San Diego's sweetheart. This was Maureen Connolly.

Endnotes

1. Dave Gallup, "Tennis Great 'Mo' Connolly Dies in Dallas," *San Diego Union*, May 22, 1969.
2. Jerry Magee, "Connolly's feel for the game made her huge on the tennis court." *San Diego Union-Tribune*, December 21, 1999.
3. Arthur Voss, "Give 'Em Hell, Mo!" *San Diego Union*, November 10, 1988.
4. Maureen Connolly, *Forehand Drive* (London: MacGibbon and Kee, 1957), 10.
5. Beverly Beyette, "The Legend of 'Little Mo'," *Los Angeles Times*, September 5, 1978.
6. Gallup, "Tennis Great 'Mo' Connolly Dies in Dallas."; Connolly, *Forehand Drive*, 12.
7. Voss, "Give 'Em Hell, Mo!"
8. Connolly, *Forehand Drive*, 14.
9. Joe Brooks, "Little Mo's Tennis Game was Simply Devastating," *San Diego Union*, June 13, 1974.
10. Roy Edwards, "This is Maureen..." *Tournament Program for Maureen Connolly Brinker Mixed Doubles Charity Tournament at the Dallas Country Club*, May 24–25, 1968. This piece on Maureen includes her statistical record of wins, losses, and opponents from 1945 to 1954. Each score represented in this essay can be found in this source.
11. Beyette, "The Legend of Little Mo."
12. Ibid.
13. Ibid.
14. Connolly, *Forehand Drive*, 27.

15. Alec Morrison, "The Magnificent Little Mo," *Sports Illustrated*, August 27, 2001. The article can be accessed through Sports Illustrated archives online: http://sportsillustrated.cnn.com/features/cover/01/0827/

16. The tournament moved to Flushing Meadows in Queens, New York in 1978.

17. Morrison, "The Magnificent Little Mo."

18. Connolly, *Forehand Drive*, 50.

19. Ibid., 52.

20. Norman Bell, "Li'l Mo Wins Third Female Athlete of the Year, Flo 2nd Again," *San Diego Union*, January 9, 1954.

21. "Young Queen," *Time Magazine*, September 17, 1951, 52. Vol. LVIII No. 12.

22. Voss, "Give 'Em Hell, Mo!"

23. Cindy Brinker-Simmons, *Little Mo's Legacy: A Mother's Lessons. A Daughter's Story* (Irving, Texas: Tapestry Press, 2001), 100.

24. Connolly, *Forehand Drive*, 61.

25. Ibid., 17.

26. Brinker-Simmons, *Little Mo's Legacy: A Mother's Lessons. A Daughter's Story*, 100.

27. Connolly, *Forehand Drive*, 78.

28. A History of Women in Sports Timeline giving all Associated Press women athletes of the year beginning in 1931 can be accessed through the web via: http://en.wikipedia.org/wiki/Associated_Press_Athlete_of_the_Year.

29. Voss, "Give 'Em Hell, Mo!"

30. Beyette, "The Legend of Little Mo."

31. Ibid., 84.

32. Connolly, *Forehand Drive*, 84.

33. Connolly, *Forehand Drive*, 84.

34. Connolly, *Forehand Drive*, 88.

35. Margaret Smith Court won the calendar year grand slam in 1970, but lost a set to Rosemary Casals at the U.S. Open and Stefi Graf accomplished the slam in 1988, but lost a set to Martina Navratilova at Wimbledon and another to Gabriela Sabatini at the U.S. Open. However, Graf is the only player to win the Golden Slam, by adding a Gold Medal from the 1988 Olympics in Seoul, Korea.

36. Bell, "Li'l Mo Wins Third Female Athlete of the Year, Flo 2nd Again," *San Diego Union*, January 9, 1954.

37. Jack Murphy, "Maureen Annexes 3rd Wimbledon Net Crown," *San Diego Union*, July 4, 1954.

38. Nelson Fisher, "Maureen Connolly Injured on Horse," *San Diego Union*, July 21, 1954.

39. Ibid.

40. Connolly, *Forehand Drive*, 101.

41. Billie Jean King, interviewed by author, Newport Beach, CA, October 10, 2007. Billie Jean King, a legend in the world of tennis, won twelve Grand Slam titles during her reign on the tennis courts from 1966 to 1975. She defeated Bobby Riggs in the famous "Battle of the Sexes" match on September 20, 1973. Today she runs the World Team Tennis league and participates in many philanthropic endeavors.

42. Connolly, *Forehand Drive*, 104.

43. Ibid., 110.

44. Beyette, "Legend of Little Mo."

45. Gallup, "Tennis Great 'Mo' Connolly Dies in Dallas."

46. Billie Jean King, interviewed by author, Newport Beach, CA, October 10, 2007.

47. Connolly, *Forehand Drive*, 113.

48. Brinker-Simmons, *Little Mo's Legacy: A Mother's Lesson's. A Daughter's Story*, 57.

49. "Little Mo Goes to College," *San Diego Union*, May 28, 1964.

50. Maureen Connolly Brinker Tennis Foundation, http://www.mcbtennis.org/ (accessed February 21, 2008).

51. Billie Jean King, interviewed by author, Newport Beach, CA, October 10, 2007.

52. "Funeral Rites Salute 'Little Mo,'" *San Diego Union*, May 22 1969.

53. Beyette, "Legend of Little Mo."

CHARLIE POWELL, 6-3, 215 lbs., won renown in football, baseball, basketball and track before he turned to the ring.

Millions witnessed his thrilling knockout over Nino Valdez, then the No. 2 contender, on a nationally televised show. It was the most exciting heavyweight fight of 1959.

NOW READY TO MEET ALL COMERS.

Managed by:
SUEY WELCH,
306 West Third Street
Los Angeles 13, California

Charlie Powell promotion poster. Courtesy of the San Diego Hall of Champions.

Chapter II

A Look at the Professional Sporting Careers of Chillin' Charlie Powell

"They say I have a glass jaw and I guess they're entitled to their opinion. But I don't agree. If I thought I couldn't take a punch, I wouldn't throw over a good job with the 49'ers for fighting." – Charlie Powell[1]

Charlie Powell is undoubtedly one of the finest all-around athletes San Diego has ever produced. He may not be as well known as other boxers such as Archie Moore or Lee Ramage or found such fame in football as Marshall Faulk, Junior Seau, Ricky Williams, or Reggie Bush, but Powell never backed down from a challenge in the ring, on the field, or even during segregation. After starting for the San Francisco 49'ers straight out of college and making an immediate impact, Charlie focused on his boxing career. His time in the ring started out brilliantly as he quickly rose higher in the rankings. Charlie managed to juggle both his professional football and boxing careers during an impressive thirteen year span; and, all of this after quitting professional baseball. In his post-playing years, Charlie has been an upstanding example for young athletes who have dreams of success in multiple sports. This is the story of Charlie Powell's professional sports career and his achievements

photo - 1948 in 9th grade

CHARLES POWELL
- Heavyweight champion
* of California*
- Def. End - San Francisco 49s

Charlie Powell, age 14, 1948. Courtesy of the San Diego Hall of Champions.

both on and off the field and in-and-out of the ring.

Growing up in Logan Heights

Charlie Elvin Powell was born on March 4, 1932, in Texas. His family relocated to San Diego after his birth. He was the oldest of eight children born to Elvin and Mae Powell. In total, the Powells had five sons and three daughters. They lived in the Logan Heights area of San Diego. Young Charlie spent much of his childhood at the newly constructed William J. Oakes branch of the Boys and Girls club in Logan Heights. Beyond participating in sports, Charlie also enjoyed woodworking. He attended Logan Elementary School, Memorial Junior High, and then attended San Diego High School, where his athletic talents would flourish. Powell: "I was big for my age. I guess I weighed close to 200 as a high school freshman…I used to spar with Lee Ramage and Archie Moore for the kicks. One day, Ramage said I was the best heavyweight prospect he had seen in years."[2] Charlie was able to provide for his family while in high school when, during World War II, "we'd give exhibitions [on Marine bases]," said Powell, "then they'd take us to the mess hall, fill us up with steaks and potatoes and butter, and we'd get to take a lot of it home. Everything else was rationed, so we had it pretty good."[3] Powell believed strongly in aiding his family and would continue to do so during his professional career. The opportunities and lessons learned as a youth in San Diego created a drive within Powell that would lead to his success in both the realms of professional boxing and football.

Stand Out High School Athlete to Dominant Gridiron Star

Charlie Powell remains one of San Diego High School's
most celebrated athletes. During his time as a Caveman (the
school's mascot is now the Cavers) Charlie won CIF honors
in basketball, baseball, football and track. It did not hurt
that by the time he got to high school, Charlie was 6'-3" and
weighed 230 pounds. *San Diego Union* staff writer Chris
Jenkins detailed, "A four-sport star at San Diego High who
would put the shot in an afternoon track meet, then scurry
over to play right field for the Cavers baseball team, Powell
never saw any reason he couldn't do the same sort of thing
as a professional."[4] As a track star for the Cavemen, Powell
ran the 100 yard-dash in .98 and is remembered for clearing
6 feet 3 inches in the high jump; he also tossed the shot put
51 feet. He was the school's center in basketball, and before
being offered a contract to play professional baseball or
football, Abraham Saperstein, the famed founder and coach
of the Harlem Globetrotters sought out Powell's services.

According to Chris Jenkins: "Fifty colleges were waving
scholarships at Powell, who graduated from San Diego High
in '52 with a dozen varsity letters over three years, and he
was particularly tempted to become the first black athlete to
enroll at the U.S. Naval Academy. But he was the oldest of eight
children, and when the St. Louis Browns [later the Baltimore
Orioles] offered a baseball contract and $5,500, Powell found
a way to help at home."[5] In high school, Charlie was known
to consistently hit home runs out of Balboa Park. He is said to

Powell began his professional football career at the age of 19 with the San Francisco 49'ers. Courtesy of the San Diego Hall of Champions.

have hit the longest home run in the park's history. After the
Browns signed him, they sent Charlie to play for their farm
team in Stockton, California. Powell played only a summer
with the Stockton Ports. He became weary of the sport after
being walked constantly due to pitchers' fear of his strength
and power. He returned to San Diego, but would be back in
the bay area soon when the coach of the San Francisco 49'ers,
Buck Shaw, arrived on Powell's doorstep – contract in hand.

Due to his age, Charlie's parents had to sign his first
NFL contract which was worth $10,000. Charlie arrived at
training camp eager to make an impression. He certainly
accomplished his goal. Powell had been a pass-catching
running back, but after an injury to one of the defensive
starters, Coach Shaw asked Charlie if he would like to play
defense. Powell, who thought Shaw was kidding, replied,
"Sure." The next week, at the age of nineteen years-old,
Charlie became the starting defensive end for the 49'ers.
It has been suggested for many years that Charlie was the
youngest person ever to start in the NFL. He was one of
very few to go directly from high school to the professional
league, but NFL Hall of Famer, Daniel Fortmann of the
Chicago Bears was fifteen days younger when he made his
first start, making Powell the second youngest player ever
to start in the National Football League's modern era.

It is difficult to detail a record of Charlie Powell's statistics
on the football field since the NFL only began to include
the number of sacks in official game recaps during the 1982
season. Defensive tackling data is also not available prior to the

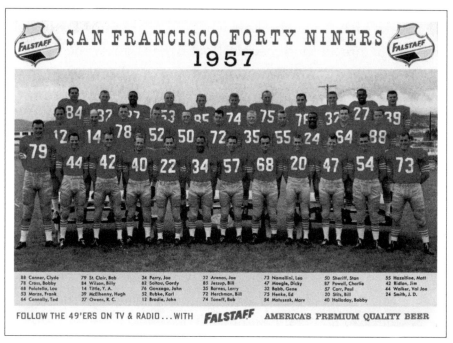

The San Francisco 49'ers, 1957, promotion poster. Courtesy of the San Diego Hall of Champions.

2001 season.[6] Yet, if Powell's career was anything like his first game, statistics are not needed to illustrate his domination as a defensive end. According to columnist Arthur Daley reporting on Charlie's first game against the Detroit Lions, "On the first play Powell burst past [Lou] Creekmur and tossed Bobby Layne for a sizable loss. It was only the beginning. Before the afternoon was over Powell had tossed Layne for losses that totaled 67 yards."[7] Powell was an imposing force that would later balance his time between football and boxing.

Charlie told Daley of an instance when he almost scored what would have been his only professional touchdown, "I'd put stickum on my hands before I left the sidelines because this

was a fake kick. Then I broke down field, scared that I'd drop
the pass before all those people. [Joe] Arenas threw the ball
and he almost threw it behind my back. I caught it, though,
and nearly had a touchdown. I was pulled down on the 3 [yard
line]."[8] Charlie took a hiatus from football to concentrate on
boxing, but after a devastating loss, he returned to the 49'ers for
the seasons of 1955 – 1957, when he once again left professional
football to focus on boxing. His next stint on the gridiron, as
an Oakland Raider, began in 1960 and lasted two seasons.

In July 1960, Charlie, who was first signed by the Los
Angeles Chargers, was traded to the Oakland Raiders.
"Powell, now 27, is back at football trying for a defensive
end or line backers spot with the Oakland Raiders of the
new American Football League. 'I'm definitely through with
boxing,' Powell said. 'You get cut up too many ways – and
I don't mean cuts on my face. The purses aren't worth it.'"[9]
Powell returned to the Raiders for his seventh professional
season in 1961 as Jack Hawn had predicted, "Powell, who
was co-captain of the Oakland Raiders of the American
League last year, still doesn't have his heart set on boxing
as a one-sport activity, and it would surprise no one if he
suited up again for the Raiders in the fall."[10] Charlie would
play two seasons with the Raiders, wearing his old jersey,
#87. He was also one of the team's co-captains. Despite his
insistence that he was done with boxing, Charlie would end
his football career before he put down the gloves. After the
1961 season, in which the Raiders finished their season a
dismal 2-12, Charlie prepared for one more boxing comeback.

A Rollercoaster Ride inside the Ring

It had been Charlie's passion since he was a young man in the Logan Heights area of San Diego to compete in boxing, just as his idol Archie Moore had done. Charlie explained to sports writer, John Hall, "I must have been only about six when my dad took me to see my first fight in San Diego and that was it. From then on, I went down to the gym every chance I'd get. San Diego had good fighters around then. Archie Moore was one of them and he took a liking to me and showed me a few tricks."[11] He was unable to participate in amateur tournaments as a youngster due to the governing body of state schoolboy athletics (CIF) strict policy against it. Powell told sports columnist Will Connolly, "I would have lost my high school eligibility if I had boxed in those tournaments."[12] His lack of experience would haunt him throughout his career. Yet, alongside his manager, Suey Welch, and trainer William "Gorilla" Jones, Charlie's preparations for a career in boxing began.

"Chillin'" Charlie was the nickname bestowed upon Powell and on March 7, 1953, Charlie got in the ring for his first professional bout against Fred Taylor. The match took place in Hollywood, California, and ended in a draw in the fourth round. It turned-out that early in the fight, Charlie had broken his hand and remarkably continued to fight with the other hand. Beyond the setback of the broken hand, Charlie had a bright future ahead of him and, in 1954, he would shine.

From February 23 through September 2, 1954, Powell competed in eleven bouts. He won them all, he won ten of them

by knocking out his opponent. On March 17, Charlie fought
Harlan Kelly in Los Angeles, California. At the one minute
and nine second mark of the third round, Powell knocked
out Kelly. Hall wrote, "He [Charlie] bounced past another
milestone Monday night at the Olympic when he knocked
out Harlan Kelley in the third round of his first scheduled
10-round main event. That made it five kayoes in seven bouts
spanning a total of only 16 rounds."[13] After the bout, Powell
explained to Hall why he had chosen boxing over his career
as a defensive end for the San Francisco 49'ers, "I've got a
family of seven brothers and sisters I want to help. I'd like
to send my two kid brothers to college. I didn't get a chance,
myself."[14] He later went on to add, "Football is more dangerous
than fighting. Maybe you'll get hit in the head in the ring,
but football gets you in the knee, ankle, leg – anywhere. I've
seen things on the field that make you sick."[15] Charlie's next
two fights would take place in his home town of San Diego.

Bob Ortman of the *San Diego Union* detailed the anticipation
for Charlie's homecoming, "Chillin' Charlie Powell, Suey Welch's
prize 22-year-old ring prospect, makes his hometown boxing
debut tonight against brawling Frank Buford in the 10-round
main event at the Coliseum."[16] Later in his column, Ortman
notes, "A near capacity crowd, including [31st California] Gov.
Goodwin Knight is expected to turn out to see if it's true what
they say about the fabulous San Diego High athletic product."[17]
The crowd was certainly proud of their native son. They had
seen him succeed in four sports while a student at San Diego
High School and now they had a chance to see their rising star

Chillin' Charlie in action. Courtesy of the San Diego Hall of Champions.

Powell celebrates with his manager, Suey Welch, after a victory. Courtesy of the San Diego Hall of Champions.

vanquish another foe – this time in person. The match was over before most of Powell's hometown crowd took their seats. Charlie knocked out Buford early in the second round. A year earlier, Buford had lasted nine rounds against Charlie's mentor, Archie Moore, in the same venue. Less than a month later, the Coliseum filled again for Powell's bout against Al Spaulding. *San Diego Union* sports writer Howard Hagen described the outcome of Charlie's second home town match, "Chillin' Charlie Powell, San Diego's newest nominee for international boxing laurels, gained his eighth straight victory of a young but brilliant professional career at the Coliseum last night by stopping bulky Al Spaulding in 39 seconds of the second round."[18] Charlie continued to dominate in the fights that followed his San Diego homecoming and even found himself being compared to greats such as Joe Louis. William "Gorilla" Jones told *Los Angeles Times* sports editor, Paul Zimmerman, "Joe Louis was a great finisher, but this kid Powell finishes you with one punch. He has quick hands like Louis and the fastest reactions of any heavyweight I have seen in years."[19]

Charlie finished off Rocky Jones in a bout in Oakland, California on July 13 in 50 seconds. Jack Fiske of the *San Francisco Chronicle* wrote, "Charlie Powell never had it so easy in the National Football League. The ex-San Francisco 49'er defensive end worked a total of 50 seconds last night at Oakland Auditorium before knocking out Rocky Jones."[20] Frankie Albert, a front office member of the San Francisco 49'ers and a famed quarterback reluctantly stated, "His [Charlie's] success in the ring makes it look like we won't have him back for the 1954 season, and we'll certainly miss him at defensive end – but all of us are wishing him great luck in the fight business."[21] Despite all of the success Charlie was having in the ring, many boxing fans at the time claimed that he was not facing any real competitors and, without truly proving himself, he could find himself being set up for failure. Sports columnist, Eddie Muller stated after Charlie's early successes in the ring, "Powell should be booked up for what he really is—a fine prospect. Well wishers can do him harm by insisting he's ready for tough ten round fights. That gives the public the impression he has everything. He's still in the developing stage. And there's no substitute for experience."[22] With a win over his next opponent, Keene Simmons, Charlie would earn the opportunity to face an experienced opponent in Charlie Norkus. Dwain Esper of the *Hayward Daily Review* noted, "This jump to the big time was Powell's reward for stopping Keene Simmons of New Jersey last night at the Oakland Auditorium in a bruising encounter before an estimated crowd of 3700."[23]

It took six rounds with Simmons, but Charlie finally beat his foe via knock out. He had earned the chance to take on Charlie Norkus. The bout was set to take place on October 6 in San Francisco and would be Charlie's first televised fight. Many of Charlie's 49'ers teammates would be in attendance. A defeat over Norkus would propel Powell's career to even greater heights than he had experienced so far. The year 1954 had been exceptional for Powell, but the Norkus bout would change everything. A sympathetic Alan Ward, columnist for the *Oakland Tribune*, described the aftermath of the fight and put blame on a public who pushed for the fight; "The former San Diego high school athletic star wasn't ready for the best. He wasn't ready even for Norkus, and certainly the latter can't be included in the country's top five heavyweights."[24] Earlier in the column Ward states, "The record book will say that Charlie Norkus scored a seventh round knockout over Charlie Powell last night...but the record book is wrong. Public opinion knocked out a young man from San Diego who abandoned a promising professional football career for pugilism."[25]

Charlie stood tall for six rounds, but was finally knocked out in the seventh round. In fact, not only was Powell knocked out in the match, he was knocked out of boxing. Devastated with the outcome of the fight and unhappy with a press and public that lost faith as quickly as they had gained it, Charlie decided to return to the 49'ers for the 1955 season. The *San Diego Union*'s Sports Editor Jack Murphy wrote Charlie's boxing obituary, "Indeed, it's unlikely that anybody will take Powell seriously as a fighter until he lived down that beating by Norkus. It was the San Diego pugilist's only showing on television and, to put it bluntly, he looked awful. Norkus not only beat Powell in the ring, but also knocked him out of the boxing business. Powell soon went back to his old stand as a defensive end for the San Francisco 49er's."[26]

Powell shared his own assessment of the fight with Murphy, "I was a smart, young punk and I thought I knew all the answers. I was more interested in having a good time than in training and learning how to fight. A lot of people were slapping me on the back and telling me how great I was."[27] Charlie's return to the 49'ers only fueled his passion to get back into the ring. He found living down the Norkus fight impossible. Even on the football field opponents would yell, "Look out, Charlie, here comes Norkus."[28] After the conclusion of the 1955 season with the 49'ers, Powell dedicated himself completely to not only returning to the ring, but to successfully defeat Charlie Norkus.

Over the next three years (1955 – 57), Charlie wore the #87 jersey for the San Francisco 49'ers while returning to the ring for a few bouts. In 1955 he competed in only two fights, a ten-round win over Hans Friedrich, his first fight since the Norkus affair, and a six-round affair with Johnny Summerlin in which

Powell trains for an upcoming bout. Courtesy of the San Diego Hall of Champions.

Powell was knocked out. His boxing career may not have been memorable in 1955, but his marriage would be. Charlie married his long time girlfriend, Irma Crawford, whom he had met while the two attended Logan elementary school. Charlie was now balancing football, boxing, and marriage. His boxing career had a bit of an upswing in 1956 when Powell competed in four bouts, winning three of them. However, the fourth fight, a seventh-round knockout loss to Roger Rischer would keep Charlie out of the ring and on the football field for the next year.

After the 1957 season with the 49'ers, Powell decided to give up football for good. George Davis wrote, "There was considerable sadness up around the Golden Gate when Charlie gave up the gridiron to become a battler. He had been a valuable member of the San Francisco 49'ers, one of the best defensive ends in pro football."[29] Powell: "I just don't want to play anymore football. It was fun while it lasted. There is no limit to how much you can make in this game (boxing). The old master (Archie Moore) started me in this game and I'm going to make it. If I hit some snag or bump in the road, that won't stop me. I'm determined. I'll make it."[30] Yet, many sports columnists were skeptical about Powell's comeback. They referred to him as "football's turncoat" and questioned why he was giving up his lucrative career in professional football. Charlie would put all doubt to rest in 1957 when he once again found himself dominating in the ring. This time, however, he had gained the experience to overcome more seasoned opponents, including Charlie Jones.

According to Johnny McDonald, "Charlie Powell, exhibiting signs of more polish, made quick work of Charlie Jones of Newark last night, scoring a second round knockout in a scheduled 10-round main event before some 1,700 fans in the Coliseum."[31] The defeat of Jones took place in San Diego, but a more thrilling match would occur only fourteen days later, once again in San Diego and once again versus Powell's hated rival, Charlie Norkus. Powell versus Norkus II took place on December 19, 1958. In a thrilling battle that went the 10-round distance, Charlie Powell defeated Norkus as well as his own demons. Charlie had reached his prime and in doing so, he earned the chance to fight the number two challenger for the

heavyweight title (Floyd Patterson held the title at the time),
Cuba's Nino Valdes. Along with Suey Welch and new manager,
Joe Vella, Charlie traveled to Miami, Florida to take on Valdes.

According to Jack Murphy: "It's suspected Charlie Powell
is about to walk into an ambush tonight in Miami Beach, Fla.
The muscular San Diego heavyweight is booked for a televised
10-rounder with Nino Valdes and it's feared the experience
may be unpleasant for Powell."[32] Murphy was not the only
one who felt that Powell could very well be overwhelmed
in the fight, but Powell had confidence in himself and saw
great opportunities on the horizon (if he could only beat
Valdes). Powell commented: "If I can handle Valdes, I'll jump
up into the ratings and be on my way. This means quite a bit
to me...I want to make a good showing for my family and
friends in San Diego. I hope I don't let them down."[33] Powell
did not disappoint his family and friends in San Diego nor
boxing fans around the world. The fight lasted eight incredible
rounds. "The one time San Francisco 49'er football player hit
him [Valdes] with everything but a machete and it was all
over after 2:03 of the eighth round."[34] Murphy, who had been
skeptical about Powell's chances, wrote the next day, "Powell
has done an astonishing thing. In just one fight he vaulted
from nowhere to everywhere. I can't recall the last time an
unranked fighter knocked over a pugilist of Valdes' stature."[35]

Charlie Powell was now at the number four position
in the heavyweight division. A rematch with Valdes was
organized to take place in Cuba. However, the Cuban revolution
occurred just months prior to the scheduled Powell – Valdes

fight. Fidel Castro, the product of a wealthy family in Cuba, became "shocked by the contrast between his own comfortable lifestyle and the dire poverty of so many others, he became a Marxist-Leninist revolutionary."[36] Castro, after a failed attempt in 1953 to overthrow the government of President Fulgencio Batista, continued his efforts. On January 8, 1959, Castro's army took residence in Havana, the country's capital. On February 16, 1959, Fidel Castro became Prime Minister of Cuba. His ascension to power created tension with the United States and thus free travel between the two nations was halted. The rematch with Valdes never took place.

Following the initial bout with Valdes, Powell's rollercoaster boxing career began a steep decline. His first fight after Valdes ended in a shocking ten round loss to Roy Harris on June 9, 1959. More shocking was the first-round knock out at the hands of Mike DeJohn on November 6, 1959. Powell's ranking plummeted—and as he had done in the past—Powell escaped back to the world of professional football. In 1960, he was signed by the Los Angeles Chargers during their one and only season in Los Angeles before relocating to San Diego, but the Chargers traded Charlie to the Oakland Raiders. In Oakland he was named one of the team captains and continued to rule the defensive line during the 1960 and 1961 seasons. In 1960, Powell only fought in one bout, a ten round match that went the distance ending in a decision for Powell. Charlie did not enter the ring for a professional fight in 1961. However, in 1962, he once again gave up football to give boxing one more chance.

In front of his home town San Diego fans, Charlie's

Powell as an Oakland Raider. Trading Card. Author's collection.

return to the ring in 1962 resembled a flash of the youthful
rising star – a flash the crowd had seen several years earlier
in 1954. Powell knocked out his opponent, Gerry Gaines
in the second round. His most infamous fight occurred
less than a year after his victory over Gaines, when Powell
faced a heralded newcomer named Cassius Marcellus Clay,
Jr. This newcomer had won a gold medal in the Lightweight
Division at the 1960 Olympics in Rome, Italy and was now
competing as a professional in the heavyweight division. Upon
becoming a professional fighter, Clay had yet to lose a bout
prior to his fight with Powell in Pittsburgh, Pennsylvania.

On June 24, 1963, the young, boisterous, self promoting,
Cassius Clay, who would change his name to Muhammad
Ali two years later after becoming a member of the Nation of
Islam, was set to take on Charlie Powell. During the weigh-in
prior to the match, Jack Olson of *Sports Illustrated* commented
that "Clay's barbed tongue seems to have brought him close
to a showdown, bare-fisted fight. According to several reports,
Clay flailed away at Powell with insults, and Powell took them
seriously and threatened to fight Clay on the spot. When Clay
saw that he had enraged Powell, the atmosphere changed. Clay
backed off, lost his composure, began to whimper and put on
his sweater inside out."[37] Angelo Dundee, Clay's manager stated,
"We're just having some fun, and we're trying to sell some
tickets."[38] In fact, the venue sold out even though it was reported
to be 12 degrees below zero that night in Pittsburgh. Over 17,000
people attended the fight that night. Charlie may have forced
Clay to back down during the weigh-in, but after an impressive

start, Powell learned very quickly that Clay could indeed "sting-like-a-bee." Powell was knocked-out early in the third round. Ironically, Clay had predicted that he would win in three.

Powell recalled: "It was a very fast fight. Clay had a good chin, good size, a lot of heart. He always said I hit him harder to the body than anybody else. I got him with a right hand. He grunted, then just stood there for a second. Everybody thought it was over. But he came out of it."[39] Unfortunately, the loss to Clay would be followed by four losses in his final six bouts. A thyroid condition he had developed contributed to his decline. Charlie's first international match took place on December 12, 1964, in San Juan, Puerto Rico, against former heavyweight champion, Floyd Patterson, whose career was also fading. Patterson knocked out Powell in the sixth-round. Knowing that he did not have much strength remaining to continue in the professional boxing ring, Powell competed in his last fight in London, England, on January 26, 1965. He took on the young British "Golden Boy" Billy Walker who had once received praise from Queen Elizabeth II. Walker made short work of Powell with a knock out in the second-round.

Powell's boxing career ended (24-11-3) with 18 knock outs. He may not be remembered in history as one of the sport's greatest, but Charlie Powell undoubtedly achieved a number of memorable victories in the ring and held his own against the boxing elite, many times, while playing at the highest level in the National Football League. What sports fans will remember is that Powell is one of the finest multi-professional sports athletes to ever compete, and he did it during an era of rapid social change and continued injustice toward African Americans. All the while, Powell competed with poise and confidence; he became a role model for future African American athletes. Powell's career inspired others to follow their dreams and not limit themselves to just one sport.

A Role Model Emerges During Segregation

When Charlie Powell began his professional football career, it had only been a few years before in which African Americans were allowed to compete in the sport. According to authors David Wiggins and Patrick Miller, "Throughout the 1950s, however, teams from both the National Football League (NFL) and the All-America Football Conference gradually added Black players to their rosters. Influenced by the enormous success of the racially integrated Cleveland Browns, owners increasingly realized that the future fortunes of their own clubs could be enhanced by the addition of physically gifted Black players."[40] By the time Charlie played in his last season with the Oakland Raiders, there were eighty-three African Americans on NFL teams.[41] "In that same year the Washington Redskins became the last team in professional football to desegregate when they signed Bobby Mitchell, John Nisby, Leroy Jackson, and Ron Hatcher."[42]

During his years playing football, Charlie was not allowed to stay in many of the same hotels as his white teammates due to the Jim Crow segregation laws. Yet, in many ways, Charlie found this to be an advantage rather than a disadvantage, as he told Chris Jenkins: "That's how I got close to the Count

Basies, the Duke Ellingtons, the Ray Robinsons. We all stayed
in the same hotels. We met in the hotels, hung out together,
became personal friends. How else could a kid get to know
people like that?"[43] Another remarkable way Charlie, along
with many African American athletes at the time, chose to
show his support for the civil rights movement was through his
positive participation in sports while serving as a role model
for what young African American men could hope to achieve.

In some cases, however, Black athletes were labeled "Uncle
Tom's" by the more militant black protest leaders for not
speaking-out with as much fervor. Jackie Robinson, like Powell,
was among these athletes. According to Dave Zirin, "Robinson
was once again a target of derision – but this time for young Black
militants and revolutionaries who saw him as a front man for a
nation and a civil rights program that wasn't responding to their
anger and urgency."[44] Wiggins and Miller noted, "Black athletes
during the civil rights era had to balance individual ambition and
collective action, a difficult proposition for a group who knew
full well that conformity and a certain deference to authority
were the typical behaviors essential for survival in sport."[45]

Wiggins and Miller point out, "Although militancy was
one approach to rectifying racial problems, triumphs by Black
athletes had actually 'reached more anti-Negro people' and
'changed more anti-Negro hearts.'"[46] Reginald Grant, a former
member of the New York Jets wrote, "The intense racial pressure
and segregation created an environment where a new breed of
socially responsible African-American emerged. They led by
example and risked their own lives to change the face of America.

Charlie Powell was one of those unsung heroes who helped knock down the barriers of racism. He just did what he did and he did it with dignity and class, at the very highest level."[47]

Indeed Charlie Powell's success on the playing field and in the boxing ring led future well-known athletes to find success in multiple sports, yet it is the combination of his passion, intensity, physical gifts, and dedication to succeed not only for himself, but for his family and as a representative of San Diego, that made him one of the great all-around athletes San Diego has ever produced. After Charlie's football and boxing days ended, Powell became a representative for his local union and started his own business in South Central Los Angeles. In 1995, the San Diego Hall of Champions made Charlie a member of the Breitbard Hall of Fame along with his brother, Art, who had been inducted in 1992.

Today, Charlie lives in Altadena, California, with his wife of fifty-three years, Irma, and continues to be a positive role model for not only African American children, but all children who have high aspirations of achieving success in multiple ventures.

Endnotes

1. Jack Murphy, "Loss To Norkus Haunts Powell As He Tries Boxing Comeback," *San Diego Union*, December 4, 1958.
2. Will Connolly, "Charlie Powell Sweats Off the Grid Blubber," *Los Angeles Times*, March 21, 1954.
3. Chris Jenkins, "Powell hit with Power in Three Sports," *San Diego Union*, February 14, 1995.
4. Ibid.
5. Ibid.
6. During Charlie Powell's career with the 49'ers, the team's wins versus losses records were, 1952 7-5, 1953 9-3, 1955 4-8, 1956 5-6-1, and 1957 8-4. In 1957 the team lost the western conference championship to the Detroit Lions, 31-27. This was Charlie's only playoff appearance. As a member of the Oakland Raiders, the team's wins versus losses records were, 1960 6-8, and 1961 2-12.
7. Arthur Daley, "Election of Professions," *Los Angeles Times*, 1956.
8. Ibid.
9. Associated Press, "Ex-49er Powell Quits Ring For Bid with Raiders," *Los Angeles Times*, July 13, 1960.
10. Jack Hawn, "World of Charlie Powell," *Los Angeles Times*, January 23, 1963.
11. John Hall, "Boxing First Powell Dream," *Los Angeles Mirror*, May 16, 1954.
12. Connolly, "Charlie Powell Sweats Off the Grid Blubber."
13. Hall, "Boxing First Powell Dream."
14. Ibid.
15. Ibid.

16. Bob Ortman, "Powell Faces Buford In Debut Here Tonight," *San Diego Union*, May 28, 1954.
17. Ibid.
18. Howard Hagen, "Powell Kayoes Foe In Second, Runs Skein to 8," *San Diego Union*, June 26, 1954.
19. Paul Zimmerman, "Sportscripts," *Los Angeles Times*, July 13, 1954.
20. Jack Fiske, "Powell KO's Jones 50 Seconds of First," *San Francisco Chronicle*, July 14, 1954.
21. George T. Davis, *"Albert Predicts Rosy Future for Powell in Fight Game,"* *Los Angeles Herald-Express*, June 19, 1954.
22. Eddie Muller, "Too Much Praise for Charlie Powell Can Cause Him Harm at This Time," *San Francisco Examiner,* July 14, 1954.
23. Dwain Esper, "Ex-Grid Star Earns Big Time Bout With 6 Round TKO Victory," *Hayward Daily Review*, September 3, 1954.
24. Alan Ward, "On Second Thought," *Oakland Tribune*, September 7, 1954.
25. Ibid.
26. Murphy, "Loss to Norkus Haunts Powell As He Tries Boxing Comeback."
27. Ibid.
28. Ibid.
29. George T. Davis, "Powell's Return to Ring Compares Football, Boxing," *Los Angeles Herald-Express*, January 18, 1956.
30. Brad Pye, Jr., "Why Did Powell Quit Football," *Santa Cruz Sentinel*, August 2, 1955.
31. Johnny McDonald, "Powell Flattens Jones in Second," *San Diego Union*, December 6, 1958.
32. Jack Murphy, "Powell Appears Overmatched But He Doesn't Think So," *San Diego Union*, March 4, 1959.

33. Murphy, "Powell Appears Overmatched But He Doesn't Think So."

34. Jack Murphy, "Powell's Astonishing Triumph Opens up a Bright Ring Future," *San Diego Union*, March 5, 1959.

35. Murphy, "Powell's Astonishing Triumph Opens up a Bright Ring Future."

36. "Castro: Profile of the great survivor," *BBC News*, February 2, 2008. Story accessed from http://news.bbc.com.uk on November 19, 2008.

37. Jack Olsen, "Hysteria Is A Sometime Thing," *Sports Illustrated*, April 25, 1966.

38. Ibid.

39. Jenkins, "Powell Hit with Power in Three Sports."

40. David K. Wiggins and Patrick B. Miller, *The Unlevel Playing Field* (Chicago, University of Illinois Press, 2003), 235.

41. During Charlie Powell's first year with the San Francisco 49'ers he was one of two African Americans on the team. The Los Angeles Rams had 7; Cleveland Browns had 6, Giants 2, Dallas Texans 2, Philadelphia Eagles 3, Chicago Cardinals 2, and Chicago Bears 1. The league had 27 African American players. By the time Charlie played his final season, there were eighty-three African Americans playing professional football.

42. Ibid.

43. Jenkins, "Powell Hit with Power in Three Sports."

44. Dave Zirin, *What's My Name, Fool? Sports and Resistance in the United States* (Chicago: Haymarket Books, 2005), 38.

45. Wiggins and Miller, *The Unlevel Playing Field*, 273.

46. Ibid.

47. Reginald Grant, "Mr. Versatility" – The Youngest Player in NFL History," *Black Sports The Magazine*, February 2006, 18.

Greg Louganis takes flight. Courtesy of the San Diego Hall of Champions.

Chapter III

Greg Louganis: San Diego's Dominant Diver

"When I started diving, it was to gain the approval of my parents. Then it was to gain the approval of my coaches. Then I dived for my country. Now, I'm diving for me. It's amazing what I had to go through to get to this point." – Greg Louganis[1]

One of San Diego's proudest sons, Greg Louganis, has lived a life full of accomplishments and praise for his successes on the diving board. Yet, Greg's well-documented story is far more complex than fans from his native El Cajon, California, as well as those from around the world, even realize. The top sports writers covered Greg's amazing career from his silver medal at the 1976 Olympics in Montreal, Canada, to his revelation that he is HIV positive after the 1988 Olympics in Seoul, South Korea, and everything in-between. Louganis's childhood became a juicy topic for reporters as it came to light that he had been adopted at the age of nine months and had his name changed.

In their articles on Louganis, columnists detailed the life of a shy young boy who was picked-on throughout his school years and found solace in diving and dancing. They noted his physical prowess, which stole the hearts of females the world over, and with curiosity pondered why he did not have

Greg Louganis wearing his silver medal from the 1976 Montreal Olympic Games and two gold medals from the 1984 Los Angeles Olympic Games. Courtesy of the San Diego Hall of Champions.

a girlfriend. It was his 5 Olympic medals, 47 National Titles, 6 World Championships, perfect score at the 1984 Olympics in Los Angeles and numerous sportsman awards on which the media focused during his dominating years. Not until Greg himself, along with his co-writer Eric Marcus, decided to bring to light his homosexuality in *Breaking the Surface*, released in 1995, did Louganis become one of the most notable gay athletes. His pronouncement would aid in opening the door for other athletes to feel comfortable coming out with their homosexuality.

Greg will always be remembered for his supremacy on the diving boards. Yet he is not just a diver and not just a gay athlete with HIV. He is not just the son of adoptive parents. He is not just an actor, dancer, writer, or dog trainer. He is just a man who does not believe in labels and has thus far lived a very exciting rollercoaster of a life. This chapter will examine the ups and downs of a truly great diver.

Sacrifices and Struggles: Growing up in San Diego

Bud Greenspan dramatically wrote of Greg's birth parents, "two 15-year-olds – a handsome, athletic, dark-skinned Samoan boy and a blond, blue-eyed Swedish girl – are talking. The girl, crying, is holding a small baby. They have become the unwelcome parents of a child they've named Tim. Unable to care for the baby, they decide to give him up to a foster home."[2] There has been much speculation regarding Greg's natural parents, but what is known is that on January 29, 1960, Louganis was born, a beautiful, dark-skinned child with a heartwarming smile. He was placed with a foster family through the Children's Home Society of San Diego. Louganis noted, "For the first nine months I lived with a foster family. The adoption agency was having a tough time placing me because of my coloring. The family that took care of me called me Timmy, which might have been the name my natural parents had given me."[3] The common belief is, according to columnist Pat Jordan, "his father wanted to raise him as a brother, but his mother convinced him it would be best to put their son up for adoption."[4] Regardless, Peter and Frances Louganis adopted Greg and named him Gregorios Efthimios Louganis.

To Greg, Peter and Frances are his parents—and to this day — he does not have much interest in meeting his natural parents. However, he does admit: "I'd like to see the similarities—how much I resemble my father. I have a feeling it would be like looking at a mirror of myself. But I'd do it somehow so that he wouldn't know it was me. That's an awful burden on someone. He chose to give me up. That was his choice. He doesn't need for someone to come up after all these years and say: 'Oh, hi. I'm your son.'"[5]

Frances Louganis was a native of Mount Pleasant, Texas, and was the daughter of a farmer. Her husband Peter, "a tough, swarthy Greek who owned a tuna-fishing company on the dock of San Diego"[6] was the son of Greek immigrants. The two met in San Diego while Peter was working as a bookkeeper for the Fishermen Marine Company in 1952. They married the next year and after five unsuccessful years of attempting to have their own child, they adopted Greg's older sister, Despina. His sister would become Greg's voice during his youth. Greg had a stuttering problem, and Despina would help him to finish his sentences. "Despina only wanted to help," Greg told Pat Jordan. "I could visualize the word, but I couldn't get it out. Despina would say, 'Greg wants potato chips, Ma.'"[7] Yet, Greg would not have his sister by his side while at school where his disability, along with his undiagnosed dyslexia, confused teachers and caused his classmates to call him "retard."

As Rick Reilly detailed in 1984, "Louganis was born with dyslexia – an impairment of the ability to read, often the result of a genetic defect or a brain injury. It went untreated until the third grade, and continued to worsen, as Louganis claims, by a teacher who was convinced the way to cure him of his stuttering and inability to read was to have him read aloud in class."[8] Greg's dyslexia was not the only fodder for classmate cruelty directed at him. He was the only dark-skinned boy in his neighborhood and was often called "nigger" even though his skin tone was based on his natural father's Samoan heritage. Life was rough for young Greg at Chase Avenue and later Fuerte Elementary Schools. However, he found enjoyment in dancing and gymnastics that he began at an early age.

Anita Verschoth discusses in a 1981 *Sports Illustrated* column that, "Despina was first to take tap-dancing lessons, but after Mrs. Louganis found Greg standing on his head, she enrolled him as well. 'I wanted my children to grow up with a little grace,' she says." Later Verschoth mentions, "By the time Greg was three he was performing in a dance-studio show. He sang *Dance with Me* while wearing a shiny black tuxedo

Photo of young Greg diving for Valhalla High School. Courtesy of the San Diego Hall of Champions.

that his mother made by hand, a top hat and a carnation in his buttonhole."[9] Along with dancing, Greg found a love for gymnastics which would ultimately lead him to the diving board. His participation in sports that were viewed as less masculine led to classmates calling him a "sissy," "faggot," in addition to the aforementioned term, "nigger." Bullies constantly abused him. School life did not improve any when Greg entered Emerald Middle School.

Greg wrote about his early drug use, "I'm sure part of the problem with my moods was from the drugs I had started taking in junior high school, starting with marijuana in seventh grade. The kids I wanted to fit in with smoked pot, and some of them were also smart. I didn't think I had the brains to keep up with them, but I could be a part of their group when I got high."[10] Even though Greg used marijuana, his drug of choice at the time was speed. He also drank. Jeff Savage noted, "He would sneak a flask of bourbon into school, hide it in his locker and take a few sips between classes. Then he would drink beer after diving practice."[11]

During his middle school years, Greg also found himself often at odds with his parents to the point where he had several fights with his dad and was sent to juvenile hall after kicking his mother in the chest. Louganis: "Mom came toward me, and I assumed she was going to slap me, so I reared back on my bed and kicked her in the chest. She stumbled back and fell against my closet doors, but she stayed on her feet."[12] Greg spent three days in juvenile hall. His parents came to see him every day. After his release and with a heartfelt apology to his mother, the two of them developed a strong and deep bond that would always remain. Peter Louganis took more of an interest in Greg's diving and even though Peter continued to work long hours and drink heavily, their relationship became more civil after the juvenile hall incident.

Greg began diving at the age of 9 at the Parks and Recreation center in La Mesa while still in elementary school. His first coach was John Anders who was also a police officer. Anders would be the first of three men who took on the task of molding young Greg into the dominate diver he would become. Louganis told sports writer, Chris Jenkins, in 1984 that Anders was "(the) one who taught me to be graceful. He always stressed that diving be like poetry. He taught me great things."[13] However, the coach had difficulties finding proper equipment in which to teach his young pupil. Louganis: "With Coach Anders, we traveled to wherever we could find a pool that had the proper facilities, which was especially tough once I started training on the 3-meter springboard and the 10-meter platform. Platform facilities were nonexistent in San Diego, and the 3-meter facilities were terrible. We spent more time driving than diving."[14] Yet, the times spent under the tutelage of Anders were some of the happiest in Greg's life. He competed in junior regional and national meets as well as the Junior Olympics. Even though things were rough at home, diving, according to reporter Linda Kay, "allowed him to travel to Italy, Austria, Sweden, enabled him to make friends in all parts of the world."[15] Greg was becoming a force to be reckoned with in junior tournaments and in 1975, Louganis would begin work with a new coach who would prepare him for a shot at the 1976 Montreal Olympics.

In 1948, Sammy Lee (Greg's next coach) was the first Asian-American to win a gold medal. During the London, England Olympics, Lee took home gold in the men's 10-meter platform diving event and bronze in the 3-meter springboard. Four years later, Lee would become the first man to win back-to-back gold medals in diving when he won the 10-meter platform in 1952 at the Helsinki games. Fast forward to 1971 at the Junior Olympics in Colorado, Lee saw Louganis dive for the first time and instantly he knew that Greg could be the greatest diver in history.

Savage recounts how Lee came to be Louganis's second coach. "Three years later, Pete Louganis took his son to Los Angeles to see Lee. The first thing Lee asked Greg to do was perform a 2 1/2 somersault tuck. 'Greg said: I don't do a tuck,' said Lee. 'I said, You got 15 seconds to do a tuck or you get your butt out of here and never come back.' He did the tuck. On his way back to San Diego with his father, he said, 'Dad, I need a coach like that.'"[16] Lee did not charge the Louganis family a dime. He did it for the love of the sport. However, he did have a few rules for Greg. There would be no tolerance for smoking or drinking and Greg would have to clean Lee's pool.

Lee, probably more than anyone, understood the cruelty that Greg had endured from his classmates. Lee told *Parade Magazine* in 1988, "How would you like to be a 5-foot-tall Korean kid living on the California coast right after the 1941 Pearl Harbor attack and every day having people calling the FBI to lock up 'the dirty little Jap spy' hanging around the local swimming pools, masquerading as a diver?"[17] Greg had only a few months to prepare for the Montreal Olympics and had to learn new dives. He moved to Orange County to live with Lee during this time in an effort to maximize their time.

Moving to Santa Ana to live and train with Lee was a positive break for Louganis who, while successful as a member of the diving team at Valhalla High School and as a coach for the women's gymnastics team, still did not enjoy being a teenager. In an interview conducted with Greg on September 11, 2008 he explained that during high school he would "ditch class and go to the beach."[18] His favorite beach was Pacific Beach where, like many San Diego high school students, Greg took up surfing. He also mentioned that he liked going to Black's Beach to watch the hang gliders and being young and shy, he was surprised to learn that Black's Beach was a popular spot for nude sun bathers. Yet, he would often times go alone. Greg told Rick Reilly in 1984 that, "In all my life, I've never really had a good time. Never gone out and had fun; never really let loose. Not once."[19] By moving in with Lee, Greg was able to focus solely on diving and earning a spot on the United States Men's Diving Team.

At the U.S. Olympic trials, Greg won both the 3-meter springboard and 10-meter platform. He earned his spot on the team and was headed for Montreal, where his life would change forever. Greg was to become an internationally known diving star. He would befriend the Russian diving team during a time when the United States was in the midst of a Cold War with Russia. He would develop his first crush on a man while attempting for the first time to come out to a fellow diver. The 1976 Olympics would set the wheels in motion for twelve years of suffocation by the media and fans all during a time in which the young 16-year-old would be searching to find himself.

Self Revelation and a Silver Medal

In what became one of the most classic battles in Men's Diving, the teenager from El Cajon was pitted against the defending champion from Italy, Klaus Dibiasi, crowned "the Blond Angel." The two men were neck and neck going into the second-to-last dive. Louganis: "My ninth dive was a front three-and-a-half pike. Not a lot of divers had been doing that one yet, and still I wasn't that consistent with it. Sure enough, I made the same mistake I'd made before: For some reason, as I was stretching for the water, I kept my head down, so it washed over – I went vertical."[20] Greg's scores ranged between 4s and 6s. He had blown it and knew that he would end up with a silver medal.

In contrasting accounts, Louganis notes that Sammy Lee instantly began to berate and belittle him for the dive stating that Greg had let him down. *Parade Magazine* columnist Bud Greenspan, however, wrote of the botched dive, "Emerging from the pool, Greg was hugged by Sammy Lee who whispered something in his ear. Louganis smiled and, though victory was out of his reach, proceeded to score the highest single point total of the competition on his final dive."[21] Regardless of what actually occurred, Greg Louganis was now an Olympic champion. He had fought hard against the four-time Olympian who began his career at seventeen. Klaus Dibiasi had the gold

medal placed around his neck, but in achieving the victory, he
was also passing the torch on to Greg.

During his time in Montreal, Greg found it difficult to spend
time with his American teammates. "I spent a lot of time with
the Soviets in Montreal because several of them were around
my age" Louganis wrote. He continues, "It didn't go unnoticed
among my American teammates that I was spending a lot of
time with the Soviet divers…this was still the period when the
Russians were supposed to be our enemies. But I didn't care
about politics…unfortunately; most of my teammates had a
knee-jerk negative attitude toward the Russians because of all
the propaganda. One of them started calling me a Commie
fag."[22] Beyond hanging out with the enemy, Greg's teammates
also had begun to pick-up on the rumors that Greg was gay. In
fact Greg had chosen these Olympics to confide in a friend.

Canadian diver Scott Cranham had been studying
psychology and was friendly with Greg. Greg had thought
Scott was gay as well. One night while walking through the
Olympic Village, Greg told Scott that he thought he might be
gay. Greg recalled, "After that day he came near me only if
there were lots of other people around."[23] Greg was hurt by the
rejection and continued to be confused about his sexuality.

In his autobiography, *Breaking the Surface*, Greg discusses
his first crush with a Russian diver whom he called "Yuri"
(not his real name). One night, while spending some time with
the Russian divers, Greg remembers, "By the time everyone
passed out it was very early in the morning, and only Yuri and
I were still awake. I had my head in Yuri's lap and I had my

arms around him and he was holding me. We had most of our clothes off and we cuddled." This was the only time in which Greg and "Yuri" were able to be together. After the Olympics the two saw one another only occasionally. Nevertheless, Greg was now confident in his homosexuality. Yet, he knew he would have to keep it a secret. In fact, in a February 1978 article on Greg, reporter Linda Kay discusses Greg's relationship with girlfriend Julie Capps, "she is a diver Louganis met at a competition six years ago."[24] Julie lived in Miami, Florida, where Greg would attend university in the fall of 1978.

Greg's return home from Montreal would be met with a new celebrity status that neither he nor his family was prepared for. As Steve Bisheff notes, "The fame came with the rush of a tidal wave and swept him, his family and many of his friends off into a territory that seemed foreign to them."[25] The attention overwhelmed Greg and in January 1977 he actually had considered quitting the sport. Yet he became accustomed to the notoriety and was able to handle the transition back into high school life at Valhalla. Unfortunately, he was not sure whether the onslaught of interest in him was due to his silver medal or was actually genuine. These were times that he found himself contemplating while surfing at Pacific Beach, when he was not on the diving board preparing for his next competition.

Greg continued to dive as a member of the Valhalla Men's dive team, and in March 1977, "walked away with the championship in the Grossmont League diving finals... and bettered the league scoring record by over 100 points in the process."[26] He accomplished this feat after contracting

mononucleosis. In 1978, Greg won his first World Championship
on the platform. He also graduated a semester early from Valhalla.

The quest for gold at the 1980 Olympics began with a move to
Miami to attend the University of Miami. Drama was his major
and his passion. Even though he won three NCAA titles during
his years in college, it was his acting that he truly enjoyed. His
first role was in the play *Equus*. According to Verschoth, "As
well as having a bit part, Greg played Nugget, one of the horses.
Attending a dress rehearsal, Frances heard her son say some
things she had never allowed to be uttered in her house."[27]
Greg's mom would end-up seeing the show four times. Despite
the press writing about there being a girl in Greg's life in Miami,
Julie Capps, Greg did have two brief relationships with men while
at the University of Miami. He had become more comfortable
with his homosexuality, but still felt too immature to sustain a
relationship.

Greg did not stay long in Miami since he began training at
a world class facility in Mission Viejo, California, with a new
coach, Ron O'Brien. Ron had been a successful diving coach
at Ohio State, but came to Mission Viejo in 1978. Whereas
Anders had taught Greg grace and Lee had focused on power,
it was O'Brien's goal to fine tune him into the powerhouse that
he would become. O'Brien also took on the responsibility of
attempting to make Greg more of an outgoing person. He told
Anita Verschoth, "I don't have to coach him technically as much
as the other divers because of his ability level...My main job is to
keep him relaxed. I joke a little. When he smiles, he dives well."[28]

In December 1980, the University of California, Irvine,

Pictured alongside his father, Pete, Greg is honored with a San Diego sportsman award. Courtesy of the San Diego Hall of Champions.

offered him a scholarship. He accepted it and continued his drama classes. Prior to starting classes at UCI, Greg worked as a bartender in a Mexican restaurant in Anaheim, California. When he did begin his course, he took a full load of 22 units. Anita Verschoth noted, "Louganis' favorite classes are classical literature and dance...it has been said that Louganis could have his pick of admiring girls anywhere."[29] It would be a meeting with Kevin Perry, who was a few years older than Greg that would change his life forever. The two moved into an apartment in Costa Mesa, California, and began a serious relationship, but one that was kept out of the media's attention. Greg's main focus was the 1980 Olympics in Moscow.

Louganis had reached a level of national and international dominance that assured him a shot at two gold medals. He had won, in 1979, all three events at the national outdoor championship (a feat he repeated in 1980), he also won the national indoor championship in 1-meter and 3-meter springboard and came in second in platform. At the Pan American games he took home the gold in the 1-meter and platform competitions. In 1980 he qualified for the Olympics by winning the 3-meter springboard and platform competitions. Louganis' dream of competing in the Moscow Olympics would be shattered when the United States declared that they would boycott the games especially since, a few months prior to the boycott, Greg had been in Tbilisi, Georgia, participating in a U.S.–U.S.S.R. friendly meet.

The event did not go well for Louganis. An Associated Press report read, "According to officials, Louganis, a native of California, was doing a somersault when he passed too close to the diving board and hit his head. He apparently lost consciousness before landing in the water."[30] Both teams rushed to the pool to help him out. He would be fine, suffering a concussion, but able to travel home with his teammates. He did manage to finish first in the 3-meter springboard.

The Boycott of the 1980 Olympics

Due to the Soviet invasion in Afghanistan, U.S. President Jimmy Carter declared that if the Soviet Troops were not removed from Afghanistan by February 20, 1980, the United States would boycott the 1980 Olympics in Moscow. Soviet troops were not removed and, on March 21, the official announcement that the United States would not be participating in the Olympics came through the wire. Along with the American athletes, sixty-five nations chose not to send athletes to compete in the games. It should be noted that several of the countries that did not compete based their decision on economic situations and not the United States-led boycott.

The Cold War, which had been calmed by détente with the administration of President Richard M. Nixon, was once again in full swing by the time the decision was made to boycott the 1980 games. However, as Louganis told Bud Greenspan, "Had I gone to the Moscow Games and come home with two gold medals, I probably would have retired."[31] Without having to compete in Moscow, Louganis was able to focus on school and continue his rule of the boards in national and international competition.

Upon moving-in with Kevin Perry, Greg was given a very special gift for his twenty-first birthday. Kevin brought home a Great Dane puppy that Greg named Maile. She made him very happy. Life was finally settling down for Louganis. With a college degree, a few acting roles under his belt, Kevin, Maile, and achieving a place as the most dominant athlete his sport had ever seen, Greg was indeed smiling more and diving better.

Springing to Stardom in 1984

It had been eight years since the United States had participated in the summer Olympics. Now, the games were being held in Greg's backyard, Los Angeles, California. During the span from 1980 to 1984, Greg continued to add to his collection of championships and honors including a perfect score at the 1982 world championships in Guayaquil, Ecuador, on one of his dives and the Sportsman of the Year award in 1983. Greg won the 1983 United States 1-meter indoor championship in Indianapolis, Indiana, two weeks after having his appendix removed.

Beyond diving, Greg was also able to pursue his passion for acting. While studying drama at the University of California, Irvine, he also became a member of the South Coast Ballet Company. Yet, his relationship with Kevin Perry became unstable and unhealthy for the two men. Their love affair ended, but as it did, Greg finally came out to his mother Frances regarding his homosexuality. Louganis wrote, "She told me that she'd known for a long time and was glad I felt comfortable enough to share it with her." [32]

After Greg won two gold medals at the 1984 Olympics, *San Diego Union* sports writer Tom Coat wrote, "Separated by eight years, scenes from the 10-meter platform diving finals at Montreal and Los Angeles are the stuff of Olympic film and legend. The common thread in each is Greg Louganis."[33] In fact Greg had been a lock to win the gold in both the 10-meter platform and 3-meter springboard. It was no surprise that he had won, however he did manage to make history by breaking the 700-point barrier in platform diving. It had never been done before.

To add more drama to the moment, the dive in which Greg chose to go for the record was known as "the dive of death." Coat continued, "He had chosen a dive, No. 307 C, with considerable risks. A year earlier, while Louganis waited on a tower in Edmonton, Canada, Russia's Sergei Shalibashvili had tried the dive, struck his head on the platform and died."[34] In fact, Shalibashvili's death had affected Greg tremendously. He had a premonition that something could go wrong with the dive. Reilly: "The Soviet diver had been close to the platform all week on the reverse three-and-a-half tuck and his coaches warned him. Louganis knew, too, since only he, the Soviet diver and four others in the world had ever tried the dive in competition. Still, there was nothing he could say."[35] Surprisingly, Greg, who had to dive after Shalibashvili, performed the same dive and was successful.

Now, here he was, in front at the University of Southern California pool competing in the 1984 games. He managed to do "the dive of death" again in front of 17,000 adoring fans. Before the dive he spoke not with Coach O'Brien, but his most trusted confidante, Gar, his teddy bear. Greg would hold Gar and sing to him after every dive. Now, as he had history in his view, he spoke with Gar one more time before making the dive, "Gar, this is it. One more to go. Don't worry. We'll get through it."[36] His final score was 710.91. It was the highest score ever awarded in the history of the sport. Greg had become immortal. The young man from El Cajon, who had been called a "sissy" for participating in diving, dance, and gymnastics, was now an American hero.

Louganis' only regret regarding the 1984 Olympic Games was that he did not get to compete against the Soviets or East Germans who had boycotted the games. Sixteen nations boycotted the games in Los Angeles. Along with the Soviet Union and East Germans, Vietnam, North Korea, Cuba and Poland were among those who did not attend. Iran and Libya boycotted the games as well, but were not part of the Soviet-led boycott. Greg decided that he had one more run in him and would eye the 1988 Olympic Games in Seoul, South Korea, where he would be considered the "old man" of the sport, as his swan song. Over the next four years, Greg's life would be shattered with the revelation that his former partner, Kevin Perry, had contracted the AIDS virus and Greg's abusive relationship with another partner would have him fearing for his life.

Upon his return, Greg met U.S. President Ronald Reagan (Greg had been offered the opportunity to meet President Gerald Ford after winning the silver medal in 1976, but had to decline). The meeting came at a time when disturbing reports regarding AIDS related deaths surfaced. Reagan's silence on the AIDS epidemic throughout the majority of his presidency led to a negative stigma on the "Great Communicator" that continues to this day. Allen White of the *San Francisco Gate* wrote, "By February 1, 1983, 1,025 AIDS cases were reported, and at least 394 had died in the United States. Reagan said nothing. On April 23, 1984, the Centers for Disease Control and Prevention announced 4,177 reported cases in America and 1,807 deaths. In San Francisco, the health department reported more than 500 cases. Again, Reagan said nothing."[37] A possible reason for Reagan's silence stemmed from the major support he received from the religious right, including the late Reverend Jerry Falwell who had claimed, "AIDS is the wrath of God upon homosexuals."[38] By the time Reagan finally spoke out about AIDS (May 31, 1987), 36,058 Americans had been diagnosed with AIDS and 20,849 had died. 113 countries were reporting cases of over 50,000 people infected. Less than a year after Reagan broke his silence, Greg found out that he was infected as well.

1988 Olympic Games and the Strength to say Goodbye

When interviewed for this chapter, Louganis mentioned that he did not have any gay athletes to look up to, since a relatively small number of athletes had come out with their homosexuality, especially in the mid-1980s. One notable athlete to come out was tennis legend and American icon, Billie Jean King. Also during an interview for this chapter, Billie Jean King noted, "I think it has always been easier for a female athlete to come out than a guy. I am not sure why, but our society appears to be more accepting of women who have come out than men. That being said, coming out is not something one takes lightly."[39] Greg had been slowly coming out to friends and family, but still kept it from the main stream media as he had worried what kind of an impact it would have on his image and career. Already he was having difficulties earning sponsorship deals the way other Olympic heroes were.

Louganis in perfect form. Courtesy of the San Diego Hall of Champions.

According to Pat Jordan, "Wheaties never offered to put *his* photo on the box. Kathryn Newton, a Wheaties spokesperson, says that Mary Lou Retton's appeal to Wheaties was greater than his at the time, according to the three criteria the company uses to pick an athlete for its box front: the individual's breadth of appeal to the public in his or her sport, a connection to championship, and a wholesomeness in the athlete's off-the-field life style."[40] Even with all the success and notoriety Greg had gained, only a few companies (Speedo, American Express, and Carefree sugarless gum) had offered him a national endorsement deal. He did however spend some time doing color commentary for ESPN during diving events after the 1984 Olympics. Louganis mentioned to Chris Jenkins, "it's like doing an extended interview...except now I get to talk about somebody else besides myself, which is nice for a change."[41]

Despite being denied the Wheaties box cover and having to hawk products from regional gym equipment companies in Kansas, Louganis was the most imposing figure in his sport. "Athletes like Wayne Gretzky, Michael Jordan, Edwin Moses, people who dominated their sport, bringing their sport to a higher level,"[42] were those who became Greg's idols. Now, going into the 1988 Olympics, Greg had reached their status in his own sport.

Greg easily qualified to be a member of the United States Men's Diving Team in 1988. As columnist Mike Downey wrote regarding the qualifier tournament, "Louganis was so far ahead of the others that he could have belly-flopped into the water like Shamu at Sea World and still won." [43] Yet, an accident, not a belly-flop, would define Greg's legacy and forever alter his life during the preliminaries of the 3-meter springboard event in Seoul.

ESPN contributor Ron Flatter wrote, "Leading going into the ninth round of the preliminaries of the springboard, he attempted a reverse 2 1/2 somersault pike. Without a strong enough jump, he hit his head on the board and fell clumsily into the water."[44] The world was shocked to see the icon of the sport injured, but as Flatter continues, "After taking temporary sutures to sew up a scalp wound, he came back 35 minutes later to resume diving."[45] The next day, Greg easily completed all eleven of his dives to win his third Olympic gold medal.

The head wound that Greg sustained caused much more concern than simply a fear that he would not be able to compete. Louganis remarked: "In 1987, Kevin wrote to tell me that he had HIV. From the tone of his letter, I got the sense he was blaming me. In the letter, he stressed that I should get tested. I did, in 1988, and I was HIV-positive."[46] E. M. Swift from *Sports Illustrated* wrote, "The TV replay of his [Greg's] head smacking the board was sensational the day it happened; it became controversial and macabre after we learned the blood that had trickled into the Olympic pool as a result of the accident contained HIV, the virus that causes AIDS."[47]

In fact Greg had been utilizing AZT, a drug that delays the progression of the HIV virus, prior to and during the Olympics. He was worried that the drug would be considered a performance enhancing drug. The AZT was not detected in his system. His final dive, in which he was competing against a 14 year-old prodigy from China, Ni Xiong, had to be perfect as he was trailing Xiong by 3 points. The scene was eerily similar to the one set in 1976 when the then 16 year old Louganis was competing against Klaus Dibiasi in Montreal.

Now Greg was the elder statesman of the sport and as he stood on the platform preparing to perform the "dive of death" one last time in Olympic competition, the collective worldwide viewing audience held their breath in anticipation. Scott Ostler detailed the dive for the *Los Angeles Times*. "Louganis threw himself off the platform and traced through the air a 2-second work of art. He signed it with a tiny splash, bounded out of the pool and waited for the judges to punch in the scores that would give him his second gold medal."[48] Unfortunately, Greg could not share the moment with his beloved Gar, whom he had shipped to Children's Hospital of Orange County to care for a young fan whose appendix had ruptured.[49] Greg was able to celebrate his final gold medal with his mother and Coach Ron O'Brien.

According to Scott Ostler: "He won the gold and he did it unaided by steroids, side bets or Disneyland contracts. At age 28, gray hair barely held in check by black dye, weight barely held in check by a no ice cream diet, Louganis won his biggest medal ever, the one that cements his name into diving history forever. He is the greatest."[50] Greg's joy would be short-lived as the culmination of an abusive relationship with his live-in partner and manager, Jim Babbitt, was coming to a head.

Shortly after coming home from Seoul, Louganis fired Babbitt (whom he simply called Tom in his autobiography). On March 28, 1989, Greg requested that a judge bar Babbitt from having any contact with him. According to an Associated Press article, Greg claimed that, "Babbitt threatened to reveal intimate information about him to the news media unless Louganis either re-employs him on new terms dictated by Babbitt or pay him 50 percent of present and future earnings 'and deed over my home to him.'"[51] Their relationship had begun in 1982 after a meeting in a bar. They began to date and eventually moved in together.

In his autobiography, Greg discusses the fact that sharing this chapter of his life was very difficult, "I've decided to write about this experience because I think it's important for people to know what happens in an abusive relationship. Maybe I'll save someone from what I've been through. Perhaps my story will give someone in an abusive relationship – straight or gay – the courage to find help and get out."[52]

One night early in their relationship, as summarized in Greg's book, Jim raped him while holding a knife to his throat after learning that Greg had been seeing other men. Their relationship had not been monogamous and so beyond the physical pain, the rape took a mental toll because Greg had felt guilty. Instead of leaving Jim, Greg stayed with him and attempted to work things out. Jim became his business manager and took over control of his finances. Even Greg's coach Ron O'Brien had concerns about the relationship. "Greg is under Jim's thumb. Jim is a very dominant person in their dealings."[53] Jim convinced Greg to fire his attorney, Wally Wolfe, and by late 1985 was in complete control of arranging all business ventures from advertising to personal appearances. They purchased a home in Malibu (where Greg still resides) and Greg continued to believe that Jim had his best interests at heart.

While training for the 1988 Olympics, Greg had made the rounds of television and personal appearances. He was providing for himself and Jim. However, prior to the Olympics in Seoul, Jim had been diagnosed with an advanced stage of AIDS. Yet, he continued to manage Greg's life to the point that he began to drive a wedge between Greg and his parents (who had divorced prior to the 1984 Olympics). After almost seven years of being in the relationship with Babbitt in which he had been raped, taken advantage of economically and emotionally and constantly lied to, Greg finally found the strength to leave Jim.

As detailed in Greg's autobiography, "Telling Tom [Jim] that I wanted to break up was one of the most difficult things I'd done in my life, a lot more difficult than winning four gold medals. Diving was easy by comparison. It was physical. Breaking up with Tom [Jim], telling him what I wanted, meant that I had to verbalize what I was feeling. I had to stand up to somebody I felt inferior to."[54] The two arranged a settlement in which Greg would support Jim for the remainder of his life. Not long after the settlement had been agreed upon and enacted, Jim died. Greg did not go to his memorial service, but did send flowers prior to his death with a note stating that he forgave him.

Greg's goodbye to Jim was not the only significant goodbye that came after the 1988 Olympics. In a press conference prior to the closing ceremony, he officially retired from competitive diving. Also, Greg's father, Peter, had been diagnosed with cancer. The two men, who shared a strained relationship for the majority of Greg's life, would spend the last few years of Peter's life together, building a strong and lasting bond as well as healing all wounds. Louganis recalled: "We talked about all kinds of things during those few weeks at home – our lives, what we'd accomplished, his illness, my illness. He talked about how proud he was of me; he called me his 'champ.'"[55]

In 1991, during a relatively short period, Greg lost his father

Louganis pictured with author, December 14, 2008. Author's collection.

Peter, Jim, his former partner Kevin, and several friends who had fallen victim to the AIDS virus. Among the losses and tragedy, Greg continued to find strength in his passion for dogs. He had purchased two new Great Dane puppies (Jim had forced him to give up his beloved Maile). He also began a positive relationship with Steve Kmetko, the E! Entertainment anchor. Greg had peace finally, and he would make sure that he would enjoy that peace for the remainder of his life. His post-Olympic life would be incredibly fulfilling, full of bliss and continued success.

Life After Diving

On August 31, 1993, Greg Louganis made his triumphant New York stage debut in Paul Rudnick's critically acclaimed "Jeffrey," which is a comedy about gay life in the age of AIDS. Entertainment columnist Liz Smith wrote, "Louganis will play Darius, the slightly dizzy 'Cats' chorus boy who utters the immortal Rudnick line, 'Some people think I'm dumb just because I'm a chorus boy. Well, I live in a penthouse, I don't pay rent, I go to screenings, and I take cabs. Dumb, huh?'"[56] Greg would later have film roles in Disney's "D2: The Mighty Ducks" as well as several independent film roles. Titles included: 1996's "It's My Party," 1997's "Touch Me" and his latest completed in 2008, "Watercolors." In the film he plays Coach Brown. "In 'Watercolors' I got to play a real bastard of a coach. It deals with coming of age, sexuality, and drugs."[57] Greg has truly enjoyed finding success in his passion for acting.

In 1995, Greg added author to his list of accomplishments as he penned his autobiography, *Breaking the Surface*. The book would be his chance to share his story, in his own words. E. M. Swift suggested an additional goal for Louganis during his book tour, "He [Greg] was unparalleled as an athlete. He carried himself with grace and dignity his entire competitive career. He was, and is, beloved by the American public. He developed AIDS, not because he was an athlete, not because he was homosexual, but because he didn't practice safe sex. That's the message he should deliver as he travels the country promoting his book."[58] Louganis had come out about his homosexuality to the world

during the 1994 Gay Games in New York City in a video that
was shown during the opening ceremonies. He was not able to
participate in the 1994 games, but would make a splash when
he returned to the platform for the 1996 Gay Games. Greg was
now a Gay Activist and utilized his celebrity status at the 1996
Gay Games to call attention to the fact that the 1996 Summer
Olympics, which would be held in Atlanta, Georgia would
feature events in Cobb County. The county had recently passed a
resolution that condemned homosexual orientation.

Louganis, who had feared the repercussions of coming out,
had supporters in the sports world after he had done so. Michael
Wilbon of the *Washington Post* wrote in 1995, "You can be a
great athlete and be homosexual. Among the famous athletes
who have come forward to say that they are HIV positive or
have AIDS, Louganis is the first man who has talked openly
of his homosexuality."[59] Beyond continuing to lecture children
on the negative effects of alcohol and drugs, he also made the
collegiate round discussing living with AIDS. He has been an
inspiration not only to those living with AIDS, but to gay athletes
in all different areas of sports, specifically, Matthew Mitcham,
the openly gay Australian diver who won the gold medal for
10-meter platform at the 2008 Olympic Games in Beijing, China.
Mitcham scored the highest single dive score in Olympic history,
earning a 112.10 on his final dive. He was one of eleven openly
gay athletes competing at the games. During an interview for this
chapter, Greg noted that it is harder for gay athletes participating
in team sports to come out while playing. "It's hard unless you're
a Wayne Gretzky or Michael Jordan. You have to rely on your

teammates for support, there is still homophobia in sports."[60]

Today, Greg enjoys participating in dog training. In 1999, along with writing partner, Betsy Sikora Siino, Greg wrote his second book entitled *For the Life of Your Dog: A Complete Guide to Having a Dog from Adoption and Birth Through Sickness and Health*. In 2002, Jill Spielvogel discussed Greg's training schedule, "Louganis teaches about four obedience classes a week, working with his four-footed clients to increase their agility and modify their behavior at Wolfpaw Dog Training in the Ventura County community of Somis, about 50 miles from Los Angeles."[61] As well as working with his dogs, acting, and writing, Greg continues to find outlets for his creative juices. Louganis noted, "I do spin and yoga. I started dancing again. I've got a hip hop class. I have to be doing something creative. Dog training is creative too." [62]

Greg Louganis' life has been nothing short of remarkable. When he doubted himself, he found inner strength, with the help of a happy song, the love for a teddy bear or a precious dog. He continued to climb the ladder even though the world below him was scary and full of unscrupulous characters. He stood on the edge of the platform and captivated the world, even though there was sadness and hurt brewing inside him. He overcame addiction and depression. Then with a deep breath, he dove and in doing so became a hero. Today, he is proud of his accomplishments, but does not want "to be remembered as the greatest diver who ever lived. I want to be able to see the greatest diver. I hope I live to see the day when my records are broken."[63] Greg is immortal and truly a son that all San Diegans should be proud of.

Endnotes

1. Jeff Savage, "Louganis not Afraid to Flop," *San Diego Union,* August 8, 1988.
2. Bud Greenspan, "The Highs, The Lows of Greg Louganis," *Parade Magazine,* September 11, 1988, 4.
3. Greg Louganis and Eric Marcus, *Breaking the Surface* (New York: Random House, 1995), 28.
4. Pat Jordan, *The Best Sports Writings of Pat Jordan* (New York: Persea Books, 2008), 39.
5. Rick Reilly, "To Louganis, Diving's the Easiest Part," *Los Angeles Times,* January 10, 1984.
6. Jordan, *The Best Sports Writings of Pat Jordan, 39.*
7. Ibid.
8. Reilly, "To Louganis, Diving's the Easiest Part."
9. Anita Verschoth, "Winging on Toward Immortality," *Sports Illustrated,* Vol. 54, Issue 72.
10. Louganis and Marcus, *Breaking the Surface,* 41.
11. Savage, "Louganis is not Afraid to Flop."
12. Louganis and Marcus, *Breaking the Surface,* 42.
13. Chris Jenkins, "Louganis Perched Alone at the Top," *The Orange County Register,* August 8, 1984.
14. Louganis and Marcus, *Breaking the Surface,* 47.
15. Linda Kay, "Louganis Stays Light on his Feet with Life of Dancing and Diving," *San Diego Union,* February 2, 1978.
16. Savage, "Louganis is not Afraid to Flop."
17. Greenspan, "The Highs, The Lows of Greg Louganis," 5.
18. Greg Louganis, interviewed by author, San Diego, CA, September 11, 2008.

19. Reilly, "To Louganis, Diving's the Easiest Part."
20. Louganis and Marcus, *Breaking the Surface*, 58.
21. Greenspan, "The Highs, The Lows of Greg Louganis," 5.
22. Louganis and Marcus, *Breaking the Surface*, 74.
23. Ibid., 72.
24. Kay, "Louganis Stays Light on his Feet with Life of Dancing and Diving."
25. Steve Bisheff, "Louganis Tells why he Almost Became Diving Dropout," *San Diego Evening Tribune*, April 20, 1977.
26. Associated Press, "Prep Sports Roundup." *San Diego Union*, May 4, 1977.
27. Verschoth, "Winging on Toward Immortality."
28. Ibid.
29. Ibid.
30. AP - Accident
31. Greenspan, "The Highs, The Lows of Greg Louganis," 5.
32. Louganis and Marcus, *Breaking the Surface*, 126.
33. Tom Coat, "Greg Louganis Already a Part of Diving's Greatest Scenes, He Continues to Make a Splash and Spread the Word," *San Diego Union*, May 21, 1985.
34. Ibid.
35. Reilly, "To Louganis, Diving's the Easiest Part."
36. Greenspan, "The Highs, The Lows of Greg Louganis," 6.
37. Allen White, "Reagan's AIDS Legacy Silence Equals Death," *San Francisco Gate*, June 8, 2004.
38. Ibid.
39. Billie Jean King, interviewed by author, San Diego, CA, October 23, 2008. Billie Jean King, a legend in the world of tennis, won

twelve Grand Slam titles during her reign on the tennis courts
from 1966 to 1975. She defeated Bobby Riggs in the famous
"Battle of the Sexes" match on September 20, 1973. Today she
runs the World Team Tennis league and participates in many
philanthropic endeavors.

40. Jordan, *The Best Sports Writings of Pat Jordan*, 37.
41. Chris Jenkins, "Louganis still Breaking Barriers," *The Orange
    County Register*, July 24, 1985.
42. Greg Louganis, interviewed by author, San Diego, CA,
    September 11, 2008.
43. Mike Downey, "Louganis Makes it Look Easy," *Los Angeles Times*,
    August 20, 1988.
44. Ron Flatter, "Louganis Never Lost Drive to Dive," ESPN Sports
    Century Biography, 2007. This article can be accessed via http://
    espn.go.com/classic/biography/s/Louganis_Greg.html
45. Ibid.
46. Louganis and Marcus, *Breaking the Surface*, 135.
47. E.M. Swift, "A Message Worth Repeating," *Sports Illustrated*, Vol.
    82, Issue 9, March 6, 1995.
48. Scott Ostler, "Louganis Answers Olympic Pressure With a
    Perfect Dive," *Los Angeles Times*, September 27, 1988.
49. Ibid.
50. Ibid.
51. Associated Press, "Louganis 'Fears' Manager he Fired," *San Diego
    Tribune*, March 29, 1989.
52. Louganis and Marcus, *Breaking the Surface*, 135.
53. Jordan, *The Best Writings of Pat Jordan*, 39.
54. Louganis and Marcus, *Breaking the Surface*, 229.

55. Ibid., 250.

56. Liz Smith, "Plunging Into N.Y. Theater," *Los Angeles Times*, August 17, 1983.

57. Greg Louganis, interviewed by author, San Diego, CA, September 11, 2008.

58. E.M. Swift, "A Message Worth Repeating."

59. Michael Wilbon, "A Platform of Grace and Courage," *Washington Post*, March 6, 1995.

60. Greg Louganis, interviewed by author, San Diego, CA, September 11, 2008.

61. Jill Spielvogel, "A Top Competitor Steps Aside for his Dogs," *San Diego Union-Tribune*, August 26, 2002.

62. Greg Louganis, interviewed by author, San Diego, CA, September 11, 2008.

63. Flatter, "Louganis Never Lost Drive to Dive."

Tiffany Chin glides across the ice. Author's collection.

Chapter IV

Tiffany Chin: San Diego's Ice Princess

"I wouldn't want my kid to be an ice skater. No way. I'd want my kid to grow, to go to college, to become a whole person. There are so many traps in skating. Once you're ensnared you can never find your way out"[1] – Tiffany Chin

In 1981, San Diego, known more for its warm weather sports, witnessed the emergence of its very own ice princess. Tiffany Chin quickly became well known on the junior ice skating circuit. Her grace and beauty on the ice took people by surprise, especially since she was only thirteen years old when she captured the World Junior Figure Skating Championship. From that title on, Chin found herself on a meteoric rise during which she became the youngest member of the 1984 United States Olympic team in Sarajevo, Yugoslavia, and then the United States Ladies Figure Skating Champion later that year. Yet, as quickly as it appeared, it all vanished. After suffering a debilitating injury that forced Tiffany to spend months off of the ice during her peak, all comeback attempts failed in reaching the potential that she had not only set for herself, but that the world had set for her.

Chin also dealt with a strict disciplinarian mother who believed, "A good mother in China is not afraid of adding pressure. She is praised because she will not miss the opportunity to instill values in her children."[2] Tiffany's mother was often criticized by other skaters' parents, the media, and coaches. Many times Tiffany was caught between praises for her abilities and criticisms regarding her mother.

Another element unique to Tiffany's career was the number of coaches she had. According to Chris Jenkins of *The San Diego Union*, "Chin began playing ping pong with coaches, switching from [John] Nicks, to Donald Laws to Nicks again to Frank Carroll."[3] In fact, prior to those three coaches, Chin had three other coaches as a youth. Despite the difficult road she travelled, Tiffany Chin was an inspiration as the first Chinese American to make the United States Figure Skating team and to win its championship in the same year. She opened the door for Asian-American skaters such as Kristi Yamaguchi and Michelle Kwan.

Chin is the most famous ice skater to come from San Diego and even though she moved to Los Angeles, Tiffany skated as a member of the San Diego Figure Skating Club for the majority of her career. This is the story of Tiffany Chin, a young girl who set her eyes on the stars. And, while she didn't reach the pinnacle for which she strived, she gave the sport of ice skating a fresh new look and set the bar higher for those who came after.

From a Garage Sale to a Championship

Born to Edward and Marjorie Chin on October 3, 1967, in Oakland, California, Audrey Tiffany Chin was the eldest of three children. Edward Chin said of the name Audrey, "We

A young Tiffany Chin at Mira Mesa House of Ice. © SDHS, UT #91:R1680-5, Union-Tribune Collection.

always loved the name Tiffany, but when she was born, we were a little timid about it, that it might not be right. So we named her Audrey Tiffany Chin. And then nobody ever called her Audrey again."[4]

At the age of four, Tiffany moved from Oakland to the Scripps Ranch area of San Diego. She showed early signs of excellence in music, dance, and sports, all elements that would aid in her development as an ice skater. Chris Jenkins details, "Chin first displayed an uncanny aptitude for the piano – and gymnastics – and ballet. Then her mother found a pair of child's skates for $1 at a garage sale. Figure skating which combines the elements of music, gymnastics and ballet, seemed to come to her as easily as everything else."[5]

Marjorie telephoned Renee Daisy, an ice skating instructor at the Mira Mesa House of Ice. Daisy told Nick Canepa, sportswriter for the *San Diego Tribune*, "I'll never forget it. Her mom contacted me for a lesson, and I first saw Tiffany on the ice hanging onto a rail. I fit her into my schedule that day and gave her a half-hour lesson."[6] Daisy continued, "It took about a month before she started to really excel. Not to blow my own horn, but my background is teaching basics to kids who are super-talents, and I got some things across to her so she could get better faster."[7] Tiffany improved very quickly. She also found a new coach.

It was the first of many coaching changes. Marjorie hired Mabel Fairbanks, an African American figure skater and coach whose incredible passion for the sport allowed her to succeed against all odds. Author Ronald A. Scheurer wrote of Fairbanks, "Inspired by Sonja Henie's performance in the 1936 romantic

comedy *One in a Million*, Fairbanks armed herself with new
skates and headed for a nearby public rink. A persistent cashier
kept telling her that colored people weren't allowed in, and a
just-as-persistent Fairbanks kept returning to the rink. One day
the sympathetic manager, who was standing nearby, told the
cashier to let the kid in."[8] Fairbanks was not able to skate against
whites in competition, but she did create her own ice show and
performed at the Gay Blades Ice Arena for both black and white
audiences. Fairbanks suggested to Marjorie that Janet Champion
would serve Tiffany's talents better. But, not long after switching
from Fairbanks to Champion, Marjorie fired Champion and
hired Frank Carroll. Carroll would be the man that would lead
Tiffany to her first international competition.

The city of London, Ontario, in neighboring Canada was the
site of the 1980 World Junior Figure Skating Championships.
Tiffany had just placed second in the Junior Nationals
competition and was poised to win Canada. However, after her
first performance in figures, in which she had issues centering
on her routine, Tiffany placed eighth out of twenty-four. Yet, the
"China Doll" as she had been nicknamed, placed first in both
of her freestyle programs (short and long). An associated press
article detailed her short program, which included an incredibly
difficult triple Salchow, "Dashing across the ice in an orange
suit with sequins, Chin claimed the gold medal on the strength
of a sparkling free skating program laced with difficult moves.
She even threw in a triple Salchow that wasn't choreographed
into the presentation."[9] It had only been five years since Tiffany
first put on those $1 garage sale skates and now she was a world

Tiffany Chin poses at Mira Mesa House of Ice. ©SDHS, UT#91:R1680-11, Union-Tribune Collection.

champion. Chin told an Associated Press writer what winning the title meant to her, "It feels a bit unusual to be a little special – to have a talent not many other people have."[10] Despite the rise to notoriety on the rink, critics began to question why Marjorie had pulled her young daughter out of formal schooling. Marjorie stated, "We kept her in a private school as long as possible because we thought it was important for her to get a regular education, but that is out of the question now."[11]

Next up for Tiffany was the 1981 United States Senior Women's Championships, which were held in her home town of San Diego. Nancy Cleeland of the *San Diego Evening Tribune* excitedly reported, "And when the Senior National Championships come to San Diego in February, Chin will probably be there, the city's first local figure skating star."[12] Steve Petix, writing for *The Daily Californian*, said of the championships being held in San Diego, "Picture San Diego as the site of a Super Bowl. Or, if your imagination is really good, think of a World Series someday being played in America's Finest City. If the thought of having either of these 'major' sporting events in town stirs the senses, then you begin to get an idea how local figure skating fans feel as they prepare for the first ever San Diego based United States Figure Skating Championships."[13]

Chin had a great opportunity to leap from junior competitions to the senior circuit in front of her home crowd. She was the youngest competitor in the field and all eyes would be on her. While practicing for her performance at the Sports Arena, Tiffany hurt her ankle and was diagnosed with a stress fracture. She was unable to compete, leaving her home town disappointed. San Diegans felt further disappointment when the Chin family moved to Los Angeles.

Tired of commuting from San Diego to Burbank, a 260 mile round trip, four times a week for a 6 am practice session with Frank Carroll, Marjorie decided it was time for the family to move. Edward was hired as an engineer at TRW in Redondo Beach and relocated to the Los Angeles area. The family moved from San Diego—never to return. In *Tiffany Chin: A Dream on Ice*, a children's book written by Ray Buck, the author describes Tiffany's new home for his young audience, "They make movies close to Tiffany's house. Many famous people live in her neighborhood. Actor Andy Griffith lives four houses away. But Tiffany does not dream of being a movie star."[14]

Yet, Tiffany's heart remained in her home town. She continued to skate for the San Diego Figure Skating Club and asked that the media refer to her as being from San Diego. Soon after their move to be closer to coach Frank Carroll, Chris Jenkins noted, "Marjorie Chin won't discuss the subject, but sources say Tiffany left Carroll because a personality clash erupted between mother and coach."[15] Tiffany began working with her new coach, John Nicks, and together they would propel the young ice prodigy from possible contender to Olympic team member.

A year after pulling out of the National Championships in San Diego, moving to Los Angeles, and changing coaches, Tiffany was back on the ice in Indianapolis, Indiana, for the 1982 United States National Figure Skating Championships. Dick Denny of *The San Diego Union* wrote about Chin's performance,

Chin looking confident prior to a skate. Courtesy of the San Diego Hall of Champions.

"The dark-haired little 14-year-old, responding to a crowd of
14,500 in Market Square Arena which she called 'really warm'
skated a strong long program to finish fifth in the championship
ladies competition."[16] She got her chance to perform with the
veterans of the sport and she did not disappoint the crowd.
Even though she placed fifth, Tiffany was the talk of the
championships. Everyone hailed her as the future of the sport.

Rumors of Marjorie's mistreatment of her daughter continued
to hinder Tiffany's development. In one incident prior to the
Chin's move to Los Angeles, Randy Harvey reported, "After
receiving anonymous telephone calls from the rink where
Tiffany trained in San Diego, the police investigated and
concluded there was no evidence to support the accusations.
Marjorie said she never discovered who made the calls, whether
there was more than one person making the claims or even what
the claims were."[17] Yet, throughout the remainder of Tiffany's
career, Marjorie would be known as "The Dragon Lady"—a
term meant to portray her strict focus on Tiffany's career and
the mistreatment that many believed had taken place. Even with
the distractions, Tiffany was able to prepare for the 1983 United
States National Figure Skating Championships to be held in
Pittsburgh, Pennsylvania.

John Nicks told San Diego Tribune sportswriter Tom Coat,
"Her routine at Pittsburgh will be as difficult as anyone's. And
she has the ability to skate it nicely. Some skaters have great
beauty, but they're not happy with the athleticism required.
Others have great athletic ability, but they're not artistic. It's the
blend that counts."[18] The blend came together as Tiffany placed

third and won her first bronze medal on the senior circuit. Coach Nicks had two goals for Tiffany in Pittsburgh, "skate as well as she can" and "make the [United States National] team."[19] Tiffany achieved both goals and would next compete in Helsinki, Finland, as one of three women from the United States. Tiffany held her own in Helsinki, finishing a respectable 9th, and with that placement, she became the 9th ranked women's figure skater in the world. Tiffany was primed for the 1984 season. That season included an incredible silver medal performance at the United Stated National Figure Skating Championships in Salt Lake City, Utah, and a spot on the United States Olympic team.

In Salt Lake City, Tiffany faced the strongest competition of her young career. Rosalynn Sumners, who had won the championships the previous year in Pittsburgh, and Elaine Zayak, who was a former world's champion and the previous year's silver medalist, were vying for the top spot on the United States Olympic team. However, as explained by Chris Jenkins, "A wondrous, sloe-eyed 16-year-old who represents the San Diego Figure Skating Club and was deemed too young to challenge Sumners and Elaine Zayak, beat both in the long program. Less than 18 hours earlier, Chin had defeated Sumners and Zayak in the short program."[20] However, the second place finish was marred with controversy. Many felt that Chin should have won gold.

According to Jenkins, "Chin was fourth after compulsories. The speculation was that she'd intentionally been scored low —not low enough to lose out on the third Olympic spot, but down enough so that she couldn't unseat Sumners."[21] Rosalynn

Sumners was believed to be the United States' best chance for a gold medal in Sarajevo and thus when Chin beat her in both freestyle performances and still only took home the silver medal, the rumors began. Foul play or not, Tiffany Chin became an Olympian with her performance in Salt Lake City and was only 16-years-old.

A Standout at the 1984 Olympics

Tiffany Chin did not win a medal in Sarajevo, the first and only socialist nation to host a winter Olympics. But, unlike the majority of athletes representing their countries at the Olympic games, she did not want to attain medal status. Tiffany told Chris Jenkins, "I have a lot of years left. I don't think I'm ready for it yet. It takes a lot of mental power to be the champion."[22] Tiffany's coach John Nicks said, "I'm not sure she wants it. She wants to be Olympic champion of 1988, but not 1984. I'm not sure I'd want her to be, either. I hope it doesn't happen too quickly. She's only 16. She's a kid."[23]

Oddly, Tiffany's goal was not to bring home a medal for her country, but to watch the other skaters, learn about the Olympic experience and prepare herself for the gold medal in 1988. Despite her interest in using these specific games as a learning tool, Tiffany was remarkable in her Olympic debut and eventually placed fourth overall. She did not win a medal, but she won the hearts of the world. Columnist Phil Hersh wrote, "She had been skating since 1976. That was Dorothy Hamill's gold-medal year. Back then, Chin didn't even know what the

Olympics was. Eight years later, she had been considered something of the darling of this Olympiad."[24]

The compulsory portion of her performance was once again her weakest. She placed 12th after the compulsory portion. John Nicks stated, "I'm sure some of our unfriendly countries were not sorry to see her down there in (compulsory) figures, because she is so good in freestyle."[25] Nicks had been referring to the strong challengers from Russia and East Germany, specifically the eventual gold medalist from East Germany, Katarina Witt, in his comment regarding "our unfriendly countries." Beyond political animosity however, Tiffany was excellent in her freestyle performances. Her short program included what had been coined, the "Chin Spin," a combination of rocking and twirling at such a high rate, it seemed as if she had a thousand arms. According to Hersh, "Her long program, skated to excerpts from Tchaikovsky's 'Swan Lake' and 'Sleeping Beauty' ballets, begins dramatically with a triple flip, a jump few women dare try and few still can execute."[26]

When all was said and done, even though she did not want a medal, she almost got one. She went from twelfth overall to fourth place. Tiffany completed her first Olympic competition only two factor points behind the bronze medalist from Russia, Kira Ivanova. In fact, the judges ranked Tiffany second overall in both her short and long program, but her compulsory score kept her from bringing home the bronze medal for the United States. As was her intention, Tiffany was focused completely on winning the gold medal four years later in Calgary, Canada.

First, Tiffany would have to learn how to handle celebrity.

Tiffany Chin had an interest in acting after her ice skating career ended. Head shot. Courtesy of the San Diego Hall of Champions.

When she arrived back in the United States, she was deemed the darling of the games. The United States media along with the Chinese media wanted to get to know Tiffany. Tom Coat wrote upon Tiffany's arrival, "With one dazzling, but non-medal-winning showing at the recently concluded Winter Olympics, former San Diegan Tiffany Chin has become a household name – even in rural New York. And, as could be expected for someone with her style and charisma, the attention has been intense."[27] The praise was incredibly overwhelming for Tiffany. Within the first week after the Olympics, the city of Burbank planned to name a street after her. The San Diego city council discussed renaming Black Mountain Road, "Tiffany Chin Boulevard." A Taiwanese news crew arrived at her Toluca Lake home in Los Angeles demanding an interview at 7 am. United States President Ronald Reagan invited her and the rest of the United States team to lunch at the White House.

With praise came criticism. Tiffany was accused of not being mentally tough enough to reach her full potential of winning a gold medal. Tiffany's coach John Nicks said, "Talent is not enough. She has to toughen up mentally. She has a sweet innocence about her. That's nice, refreshing, but she also needs to develop…I don't know what you'd call it…She's not the killer she has to be."[28] Chris Jenkins detailed, "The picture of a delicate flower like Chin gnashing her teeth at opponents is inconceivable. Nor is that the desired result. Yet it was partially the idea of making Tiffany more competitive that the Chins changed coaches two years ago."[29] The competitiveness, in which coach Nicks and mother Marjorie had been hoping would develop in Tiffany, certainly began to shine during her performance at the 1985 United States National Championships in Kansas City, Missouri.

Whereas the Olympics had been a learning lesson, the Championships in Kansas City would be her opportunity to put what she had learned to the test and emerge the victor. The pressure from her coach and mother became more intense during the months leading up to the competition. Tom Coat wrote, "At Kansas City, she could become the first Chinese American to win the U.S. Ladies championship. And Marjorie, who along with noted coach John Nicks guides Tiffany's fortunes, is not about to let her daughter forget her Oriental roots."[30] Whereas Marjorie had taken a back seat at the Olympic Games and was resigned to being a spectator (more-or-less), her involvement in preparing Tiffany for the 1985 Nationals and World's competitions became more intense. In discussing the world championships, Marjorie expressed concern over the Japanese competition, "The Japanese skaters are willing to sacrifice anything to win. They don't have the distractions we do."[31]

Marjorie Chin was born in Mainland China in 1940. Her father was an officer in Chiang Kai-shek's army. When Marjorie was 9-years-old, the communist Red Army led by Mao Zedong defeated Chiang Kai-shek's forces. Chiang Kai-shek retreated to Taiwan. Two years later, Marjorie's family also relocated to Taiwan. Earning the chance to study at the University of Southern California in Los Angeles, Marjorie left Taiwan for California at the age of twenty-one. She believed strongly in sticking to her Chinese heritage and raising her children the way

Tiffany poses. Courtesy of the San Diego Hall of Champions.

her parents had reared her. Marjorie told Randy Harvey, "Where I come from, a mother's role is respected. If we see a mother in China get mad at a child, we normally presume that the child did something wrong. We're not so quick to presume the mother is wrong."[32] As Tiffany's career progressed after the Olympics, Marjorie's reputation continued to decline within the skating world and many felt that Marjorie's over bearing presence would cost Tiffany the chance to reach her potential.

As she took the ice in Kansas City, Tiffany did so as a member of the San Diego Figure Skating Club. She had a lot of pride in San Diego and wanted to win the national championship for her home town. Yet, as Marjorie Chin told Tom Coat, "We want to win this national championship for San Diego. This one is for San Diego. After that, well, I don't know who Tiffany will be skating for, but it's time to move on."[33] The city, that only a year earlier wanted to rename one of its streets after her, would root for her, but also knew that Kansas City could be the final time that she skated for her hometown San Diegans. John Nicks said prior to the championships, "Tiffany is number one in the country right now. If she wins, it will set her up for the future. If not, it's not a tragedy, but it is a step backward from which she'd have to recover."[34] Fortunately for Tiffany and her fans in San Diego, she won the gold medal and found herself at the height of her career, a height to which she would not return.

Tiffany was America's hope to defeat the East German representative and defending World Champion, Katarina Witt, as well as the Russian who edged her out of a bronze medal at the Sarajevo Olympics, Kira Ivanova. The people of

China were also looking to her to become the first female of
Chinese decent to win a world championship. Things started
out very well for Tiffany at the 1985 world championship in
Tokyo, Japan. The home town Japanese crowd was cheering
for Chin as one of their own, since their star Midori Ito had
withdrawn. Upon the start of the final four-minute free skate,
her strongest of the formats, Tiffany led Witt and only trailed
Ivanova by a small margin. However, as John Mossman wrote,
"She uncharacteristically turned one triple jump into a single
and fell on her final jump, a double axel. Witt moved ahead of
her to win the gold and Ivanova took the silver."[35] Katarina had
actually stood at the barrier and watched Chin's performance,
a rarity for skaters. The gold medal that seemed within Chin's
reach was substituted for a bronze.

Tiffany Chin was the United States Champion and third in
the world after the event in Japan, but Tiffany's next challenge
would not take place on the ice, it would occur in her own
living room. Shortly after the world championships, Marjorie
noticed there was something very wrong with her daughter.
E.M. Swift of *Sports Illustrated* noted, "Tiffany's mother, an
iron-willed lady whose actions have raised eyebrows in
skating circles on more than one occasion, had detected a
flaw in Tiffany's muscle development. From the waist down
everything was canted inward – Chin was knock-kneed and
pigeon-toed – to the extent that she couldn't 'cross her legs
like a lady,' never mind jump properly."[36] With the utilization
of a CBEX machine, which monitors muscle strength, it was
discovered that Tiffany had an imbalance in her muscles of

22 degrees. As Richard Hoffer of the *Los Angeles Times* notes, "Anything more than 8 or 9 degrees is considered trouble. Average is 3-4 degrees."[37] Marjorie made the decision to hang up Tiffany's skates and begin a rigorous therapy program in the hopes that Tiffany would overcome the muscle imbalance, continue to compete, and make it to the 1988 Olympics.

Rehabilitation and an Attempted Comeback

In an effort to rehabilitate Tiffany, the muscles in her lower extremities that had become weak needed constant attention and redevelopment. As documented by John Mossman, "With Marjorie supplying the resistance, Tiffany strains to redevelop the atrophied muscles. She also works with weights. The exercises are boring, but they do them three hours a day. The problem didn't occur overnight, and neither would the cure. This comes on top of five-to-six hours of skating each day and correspondence courses from the University of California."[38]

Tiffany spent seven months away from training and withdrew from several important national and international competitions. Yet, with the same vigor that she had as a youth first learning the sport, Tiffany set her sights on correcting the imbalance and continued to follow her dream. Prior to resuming her competitive training, Tiffany once again changed coaches. According to E.M. Swift, "When she resumed serious training after a seven-month layoff, Tiffany had to relearn the sport. The situation became further unsettled when the Chins changed coaches, leaving John Nicks in favor of Denver-based Don Laws

– Scott Hamilton's former mentor – purportedly to improve Tiffany's jumping."[39] Marjorie moved with her daughter to Denver and with Law's guidance, Tiffany began her road back.

She faced her first challenge at the 1986 United States National Figure Skating Championship in Uniondale, New York. Tiffany's fiercest competition came from Debi Thomas, a Stanford University pre-med student and the first African American vying for the gold medal. Debi had won the silver medal in 1985. Early in the competition, Chin did not represent her former self and struggled though the compulsory part of the program. Tiffany finished second to Thomas with up-and-coming 18-year-old Caryn Kadavy on her heels. Marjorie's stalking presence made Tiffany's attempt to retain her title more difficult. Marjorie was constantly overheard yelling at Tiffany during practice and during a television interview with John Tesh, Marjorie halted the interview and began to berate Tiffany in front of the camera crew for being "lazy," "phony," and "not worth the money spent on her training."[40] Yet, going into the final freestyle, the three skaters were close.

E. M. Swift summarized Tiffany's final performance of the championships, "Chin skated first. In the opening moments, she singled out of a planned triple flip, and her chances of retaining the title went pfffft. Afterward she seemed resigned to her third-place finish [Kadavy won the silver]. 'I'm pleased with what I did because you don't know how bad it could have been. We've got six weeks until the worlds.'"[41] Prior to the event, Marjorie made a comment to John Mossman regarding Tiffany's potential title loss, "She's the defending champion, but if she doesn't win, I would hope the skating world looks on this not as a failure, but as a courageous comeback."[42] With her third place finish, Tiffany would have another shot at redemption during the 1986 world championships in Geneva, Switzerland. This time she would be facing not only Witt, the defending champion, but Thomas the new United States champion.

Jerry Crowe of the *Los Angeles Times* wrote of Tiffany after the United States championships, "She wasn't up and coming anymore, but neither was she over and out. Thomas may have taken her title, but her spirit remained."[43] Chin told Crowe, "I always thought, if I lost my title, I would just be devastated. I would not be able to get through it. I had read all these stories of people who pushed through it, but I didn't think I could."[44] The world championship proved to be too much for Tiffany. She finished third for a second year in a row, but this time the champion was not Witt, who finished second, but Thomas who became the first African American world's figure skating champion. Tiffany had one more chance to attain her goal of making the 1988 United States Olympic team. She would attempt to overcome all the odds and reclaim her United States National title at the 1987 U.S. championships in Tacoma, Washington.

After the world championships, Tiffany released Coach Don Laws and returned to her former coach, John Nicks. She also continued her muscle training therapy for three hours each day. In addition, she also ceased to represent the San Diego Figure Skating Club. Her last chance to make the dream of standing on top of the podium in 1988 would require her finest performance and the struggle of continued therapy. It would also require that she return to Frank Carroll, the coach with whom she had the most success.

Chin rehired Carroll prior to the championships in Tacoma. Of Tiffany's muscle imbalance, Carroll told Jerry Crowe, "She seems to understand that she's got her problems and that she's got to go about it very businesslike and not get all that emotional about it. No one really cares how much trauma is going on when they're holding up the marks for you. Maybe the whole world wants to cry for you, but those judges are sitting there giving marks and analyzing what you're doing, not what you've gone through."[45] Tiffany rededicated herself and when she took the ice in Tacoma, she did so with a renewed passion and desire. Chris Jenkins mused, just prior to the commencement of the championships, "Indeed, if such a thing as open competition exists in this most subjective of sports, the senior ladies division is expected to be the best event in the Tacoma Dome this week. The women begin with compulsory figures today, skate their short programs Friday and conclude with the long program Saturday."[46]

The compulsory program, historically Tiffany's weakest element in the program, once again proved to be her downfall. After the short performance, Tiffany was in fourth place with one more chance to earn a spot on the United States Olympic team. Tom Coat wrote, after Tiffany's final freestyle performance, "For San Diegans, who in 1983 and '84 had seen an elfish Tiffany Chin emerge from nowhere to finish fourth in the Olympics in Sarajevo, the picture of a mature Chin falling or pulling out of triple jump after triple jump in Saturday's freestyle was a stunningly disappointing anti-climax to a career begun so grandly."[47] Marjorie said after Tiffany ended the competition in fourth place, "She can come back, if she decides she wants to. There's the Sports Festival next summer, and one or two international meets in the fall and then the Nationals next year."[48] However, realizing that she would not be performing at the 1988 Olympics nor achieving her dream of winning the gold medal at those games, Tiffany chose to retire from amateur ice skating.

Retirement and Legacy

Tiffany's training had cost the Chin family over $200,000. With retirement, the ability to pay them back came when she signed a contract with Holiday on Ice. "Tiffany Chin has retired from competitive figure skating and signed a two-year contract valued at more than $1 million with Holiday on Ice. Chin, 20, formerly of San Diego, had suffered from physical problems which have prevented her from regaining the form that enabled her to twice finish third in the world championships."[49] Tiffany also returned to education and earned her high school diploma. Subsequently, she attended the University of California, Los Angeles, where she studied English. Chin thanked her Chinese culture for keeping her family together during the difficult times of her comeback. "Thank goodness for our Chinese culture. If not for that, maybe we would have gone our separate ways. But I'm still close to my family. Now, I'll do the show, and I'll get my education, and I'll have my own life afterward. A lot of people who have been in skating can't say that."[50]

Ten years after retiring, Tiffany married Steven Kan and the two of them welcomed a son, Kyle, in 2004. Prior to becoming a mother, Tiffany coached several Asian-American figure skaters, including Bebe Liang who has ranked as high as 10th in the world. Of coaching, Tiffany stated in a recent interview with Lois Elfman, "I know from personal experience that this is a journey towards excellence. I would love to be that positive force who helps them through the bumps – the good times and the bad times."[51] Today, Tiffany continues to coach figure skating, while raising Kyle. Marjorie lives near Tiffany and Steve's home in Rancho Palos Verdes Estates, California and sees them often. "My mother is a very strong personality and an immigrant, so I think a lot of things she said or things that were reported were so often taken out of context. She is the person who loves me, has always loved me and I have always known that. We have a very close relationship."[52]

Tiffany Chin may not have been able to meet the highest expectations that were placed on her at such a young age, but she did, for a brief moment, capture the world's attention. In doing so, she broke down the barriers for the Asian-American figure skaters whom she preceded, chiefly among them, Kristi Yamaguchi and Michelle Kwan. Yamaguchi won the Olympic gold medal in 1992 at the Albertville, France, games as well as two world championships and one United States championship. Kwan followed Yamaguchi by becoming one of the most dominant female figure skaters ever to take the ice. She won an impressive nine United States championships, five world championships, a silver medal at the 1998 Winter Olympics in Nagano,

Japan and a bronze in Salt Lake City, Utah at the 2002 Winter Olympics. There is no doubt that Tiffany's success opened the door for Yamaguchi and Kwan. And, even if she herself never received the honor to stand upon an Olympic podium, Tiffany Chin's accomplishments gave San Diego their one and only ice princess.

Endnotes

1. Randy Harvey, "On the Chin," *Los Angeles Times*, January 25, 1988.
2. Ibid.
3. Chris Jenkins, "Chin Up, She Says," *The San Diego Union*, February 4, 1987.
4. Bob Ottum, "Guaranteed to Keep the Chin Up," *Sports Illustrated*, Vol. 62, Issue 5, February 4, 1985.
5. Chris Jenkins, "Cold blood comes hard to Tiffany," *The San Diego Union*, January 1, 1984.
6. Nick Canepa, "Tiffany Chin: From Mira Mesa to the upper echelon," *San Diego Tribune*, February 4, 1984.
7. Ibid.
8. Ronald A. Scheurer, "Breaking the Ice: The Mabel Fairbanks story," *American Visions*, December – January, 1997. This article was accessed via http://findarticles.com/p/articles/mi_m1546/is_n6_v12/ai_20084308/pg_1, on November 24, 2008.
9. Associated Press, "San Diego's Tiffany Chin Wins World Skating Title," *The San Diego Union*, December 14, 1980.
10. Associated Press, "Chin Enjoys Status of Being 'Special'," *The San Diego Union*, December 14, 1980.
11. Nancy Cleeland, "At age 13, Tiffany Chin already had shown she's more than just a good skate," *San Diego Evening Tribune*, December 10, 1980.
12. Ibid.
13. Steve Petix, "San Diego to host U.S. skating event," *The Daily Californian*, January 31, 1981.
14. Ray Buck, *Tiffany Chin: A Dream on Ice* (Chicago: Childrens Press,

1986), 12.

15. Jenkins, "Cold blood comes hard to Tiffany."

16. Dick Denny, "Chin 5th in Skating Finals," *The San Diego Union*, February 3, 1982.

17. Harvey, "On the Chin."

18. Tom Coat, "She's Growing up, so are the Skates," *San Diego Tribune*, February 14, 1983.

19. Ibid.

20. Chris Jenkins, "Chin upstages ice queens, finishes 2nd," *The San Diego Union*, January 22, 1984.

21. Jenkins, "Cold blood comes hard to Tiffany."

22. Ibid.

23. Ibid.

24. Phil Hersh, "Chin's question: Time not Talent," *Independent Press Service*, March 1, 1984.

25. Ibid.

26. Ibid.

27. Tom Coat, "Chin beckons, and the world comes running," *San Diego Tribune*, February 27, 1984.

28. Jenkins, "Cold blood comes hard to Tiffany."

29. Ibid.

30. Tom Coat, "The demands build on Chin," *San Diego Tribune*, January 26, 1985.

31. Ibid.

32. Harvey, "On the Chin."

33. Coat, "The demands build on Chin."

34. Ibid.

35. John Mossman, "Chin skating on a thin edge at national finals,"

San Diego Tribune, February 3, 1986.
36. E.M. Swift, "Books or Blades, There's No Doubting Thomas," *Sports Illustrated*, Vol. 64, Issue 7, February 17, 1986.
37. Richard Hoffer, "The Comeback of Tiffany Chin," *Los Angeles Times*, December 14, 1985.
38. Mossman, "Chin skating on a thin edge at national finals."
39. Swift, "Books or Blades, There's No Doubting Thomas."
40. Tiffany Chin interview with John Tesh prior to the 1986 world championships in Geneva, Switzerland, can be accessed via http://www.youtube.com/watch?v=m5W5EQqXBMU the interview was accessed for this chapter on November 24, 2008.
41. Ibid.
42. Mossman, "Chin skating on a thin edge at national finals."
43. Jerry Crowe, "Comeback at Tiffany's," *Los Angeles Times*, February 1, 1987.
44. Ibid.
45. Ibid.
46. Jenkins, "Chin Up, She Says."
47. Tom Coat, "A turning point for Trenary," *San Diego Tribune*, February 9, 1987.
48. Ibid.
49. Associated Press, "Holiday on Ice signs Chin to 2-year, $1 million pact." *The San Diego Union*, October 3, 1987.
50. Harvey, "On the Chin."
51. Lois Elfman, "Behind the scenes of figure skating: Tiffany Chin's love of skating continues," www.icenetwork.com, March 6, 2008.
52. Ibid.

Adrian manned first base for Team Mexico in the first World Baseball Classic, 2006. Author's collection.

Chapter V

Adrian Gonzalez: From Little League in Tijuana to First Base at Petco Park

"My dreams of playing for the Padres go back to Qualcomm Stadium. I remember celebrating beating University (High) at Qualcomm in a CIF championship game and wondering what it would be like playing for the Padres on that field."[1] – Adrian Gonzalez

Adrian Gonzalez did not have the chance to play as a San Diego Padre at Qualcomm Stadium. Yet, after being traded to the Padres in 2006 by the Texas Rangers, Gonzalez now plays first base at Petco Park. Adrian's journey to become a Padre led him to numerous minor league and big league stops along the way. He traveled many miles to end up just a few from the city in which he was born and the neighboring country in which he was raised. Along the road back to San Diego, Adrian found love in marriage and faith, each element aiding immensely in his development as a professional baseball player and as a human being. He is one of the most popular Padres players, due not only to the fact that he was a dominant high school athlete at Eastlake High in Chula Vista, California, but also because he spent his childhood moving several times across the U.S.–Mexican border at Tijuana.

Mexican communities both within the United States and
Mexico have embraced the Padres, and the organization has
supported them as well with several community outreach
programs. One program in particular has been the building of
"Little Padres Parks" in San Diego County and Baja California.
According to the Padres website, "These parks are found all over
San Diego County from Oceanside to the South Bay, as far north
as Lake Elsinore, east to El Centro and even south of the border
in Tijuana – with more on the way. Parks have been dedicated
in honor of Jackie Robinson, San Diego native Ted Williams,
Hall of Famer Dave Winfield and Andres Berumen, the first
Tijuana native to pitch for the Padres."[2] With Adrian and his
older brother Edgar on the team, a sense of pride for two athletes
that each nation claims as their own, further strengthens the
bond between the team and the Mexican community. This is the
story of an ambitious young baseball player who has enjoyed
positive success as well as having dealt with difficult hardships
in pursuit of his dream. It is also a look at a man who has found
tremendous strength in faith and family, a ballplayer who gives
back to both his American and Mexican communities, and
a native San Diegan who prides himself on his roots and his
heritage.

Crossing the Long Traffic Stop

Adrian Gonzalez was born to Alba and David Gonzalez on
May 8, 1982, at the University of California San Diego Hospital.
He was the youngest of three boys. His brothers, David and

Edgar, would serve as vital inspirations for young Adrian along with his father who had grown up in Mexico and played for the Mexican National team in the Pan Am Games. When Adrian was two years old, the family moved across the border into Tijuana, Mexico. According to Adrian, "The reason we moved to Mexico was my parent's occupations. They both owned their business in Tijuana and it was more convenient for them."[3] Adrian enjoyed the eight years he spent in Tijuana. He played baseball and soccer, enjoying the goalie position. He felt that the atmosphere in which he was growing up was more "laid back." Yet, within the laid back environment, a spark of competitive spirit was ignited within Adrian the first time he played T-ball as a youth in Mexico. According to *San Diego Union-Tribune* sportswriter Kirk Kenney, "He [Adrian] misplayed a ground ball that cost his team the game. Afterward, he went home, got a tennis ball and spent hours throwing it against a wall and fielding grounders. He did not misplay a ball the rest of the season."[4]

Adrian's passion for the sport of baseball developed while in Mexico, but when he was eleven, David and Alba decided to move the family to Chula Vista so that their boys could attend high school and university in San Diego. Of the move, Adrian said, "It was important for my parents that we attended a university on this side of the border."[5] The Gonzalez family moved to Chula Vista where the boys would receive the education that their parents had wanted.

Now living in the United States, Adrian's life was centered around sports and schoolwork. He continued to play little league in Tijuana as well as in San Diego. The baseball season in Mexico takes place during the winter and spring months, while in the United States, it is played in summer and fall. Therefore, Adrian played baseball year round. According to Adrian's biography on his website, "At times when I had games on both sides of the border in the same day, I would change my uniform in the car crossing the border."[6] The border, as Adrian told Bill Center, "was a long traffic stop. We went back and forth so many times that we didn't give it much thought."[7] During his years in middle school, he became friendly with a fellow classmate named Betsy. He didn't know it then, but in a few short years, she would become his wife. They began to date in high school at Eastlake where Adrian excelled in academics, in football, and most impressively, in baseball.

Both of his brothers had graduated from Eastlake and played on the baseball team. Adrian's oldest brother, David, went on to play baseball for Point Loma Nazarene. He won the Most Valuable Player award during one of his seasons, but an unfortunate arm injury ended his major league aspirations. Edgar played short stop for San Diego State University, and in 2000, signed with the Tampa Bay Devil Rays. David and Alba's purpose for moving their boys to the United States had been fulfilled. Both David, Jr. and Edgar attended highly-respectable universities while their youngest son, Adrian, was assisting Eastlake High to the CIF championship and being noticed by baseball scouts. Kirk Kenney wrote, "Baseball America rates the Eastlake High first baseman as the best pure hitter in the nation. Local scouts are calling him the best high school hitter from San Diego since Ted Williams."[8]

During one notable game as an Eastlake Titan, Adrian led his team to victory versus the Sultans of Santana High, earning the chance to play for the CIF Division II championship. It was the first time that Eastlake High had made it out of the first round of the playoffs. Adrian's teammate Tony Perez had high praise for Gonzalez after the game, "Adrian is unbelievable. I've been the team MVP the last two years. But I'll be glad to give him the award this year. I'll present it to him. In fact, he can have my award from last year."[9] Adrian and the Titans eventually did beat San Diego High for the championship on June 1, 1999. A year later, Adrian waited nervously to hear his name during the Major League Baseball draft.

David Gonzalez (no relation) was Adrian's high school coach. Prior to the 2000 draft, Coach Gonzalez told Kirk Kenney that Adrian was the "best first baseman in San Diego at any level."[10] He went on to say, "He's an even better person than player. He has a 3.5 GPA. He is no-maintenance. And he works harder than everybody else."[11] Adrian was one of the country's top prospects within a sea of San Diego talent that would dominate the 2000 draft—including his brother Edgar. Asked about the possibility of being drafted before Edgar, Adrian said, "People say I'm better than Edgar now. I don't think so. I think Edgar has way more talent than I do. If I go higher in the draft, it just means scouts saw something in me they didn't see in him."[12] Adrian did go higher than Edgar. He was selected number one overall by the Florida Marlins. Adrian was the first infielder since Alex Rodriguez in 1993 to earn the distinction of the number one pick. Kenney detailed the moment, "He [Adrian] signed with the Marlins within an hour of being drafted, agreeing to a $3 million signing bonus. Gonzalez graduates from Eastlake on June 16 and will report three days later to Florida's Gulf Coast League team in Melbourne, Fla."[13] Beyond Adrian, San Diego was well represented in the first round of the 2000 draft. Five players total from San Diego County were taken in the first round. No other city (or area in the country) had as many representatives. Unfortunately, Edgar did not join his brother in the first round. He had to wait until round thirty to hear his name called. Still it was remarkable to have two brothers selected in the same draft.

San Diego State University had offered Adrian a scholarship prior to his being drafted. However, as Gonzalez said, "They offered the money, and I said 'I'll take it.' I've always said the first chance I get to play pro ball, I'm going to take it. This was my first chance and I took it. I don't care about the money."[14] Adrian returned to Eastlake High during the finals week, a millionaire, a professional baseball player, and a recently turned 18-year-old. Al Avila, vice president of scouting for the Marlins said, "We all agreed that Adrian Gonzalez was the best hitting prospect available in this year's draft. Every time I went to see him, he hit. He definitely possesses the best pure stroke in this year's draft. He is an outstanding first baseman with a tremendous makeup. He has an excellent baseball background and for someone who just turned 18, he has exceptional experience and leadership abilities."[15] Adrian's incredible high would unfortunately be followed by several years of battling through the minor league system and overcoming a wrist injury that nearly cost him his career.

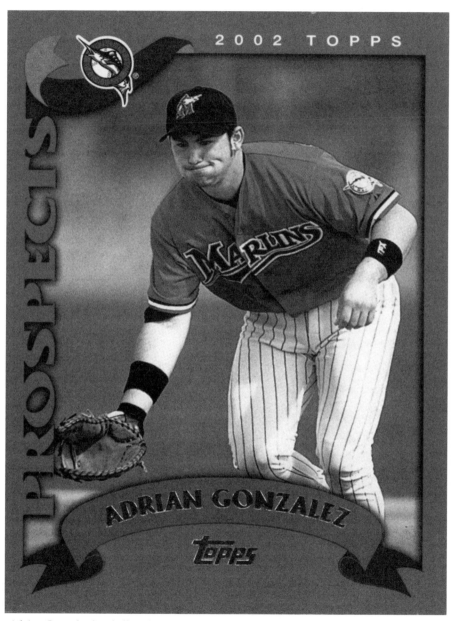

Adrian Gonzalez baseball card as a member of the Florida Marlins organization, 2002. Author's collection.

Adventure in the Minor Leagues

The Florida Marlins were elated with their new young star. They sent him to their rookie classification league team, the Melbourne Marlins, in Melbourne, Florida. He played with the Marlins in the Gulf Coast League for 53 games, hitting .295 with 10 doubles, 30 RBIs, and no home runs. Adrian then moved up one rung on the minor league ladder to the Utica Blue Sox of Utica, New York. The Blue Sox are members of the short season single A division. Adrian played only eight games with the Blue Sox and had a batting average of .310—but with only 3 RBIs. The team was later purchased by Cal Ripken Jr. and moved to Maryland. They are now called the Aberdeen IronBirds. Everyone viewed Gonzalez as one of the best first base prospects in the minor leagues.

Over the next two seasons, Adrian continued his ascension through the minor leagues, fine tuning his swing and awaiting his turn to play in the big leagues. In 2001, Adrian was the first baseman for the Kane County Cougars in Geneva, Illinois. The team was a Single-A, full-season team. Adrian played the entire season in Geneva and received numerous accolades for his accomplishments including "Most Valuable Player of the Midwest League" after leading the Cougars to the league's championship. The Marlins then named him their Organizational Player of the Year. He was also selected to participate in the All-Star Futures Game. Adrian was back on the east coast in 2002 for his third full minor league season. He was now in Double-A, playing for the Portland Sea Dogs in

Portland, Maine. At the end of the season, he was first on the team in games played, at-bats (508), hits (135), doubles (34), home runs (17), RBIs (96), and slugging percentage (.437).[16]

Adrian began the 2003 year as a member of the Triple-A Albuquerque Isotopes in Albuquerque, New Mexico. Gonzalez played 39 games for the Isotopes before being demoted back to a Double-A team, the Carolina Mudcats. During his short time in New Mexico however, Adrian found strength and a renewed devotion to religion after marrying his high school sweetheart, Betsy. According to Adrian, "I gave my life to Christ for the first time. My wife, already a believer, gave her life to Christ at the same time as well. Since that day my thoughts and actions have taken a complete turnaround. In turn, my life has been saved thanks to the promises of love and salvation I'm promised by God."[17] He later states, "Life, baseball and everything is God given and if not for him we wouldn't be here."[18]

Betsy and Adrian moved to Zebulon, North Carolina, for a 36-game stint with the Mudcats in the Southern League. As soon as they arrived, the Gonzalez's were packing their bags and heading back west to Frisco, Texas, where Adrian became a member of the Frisco RoughRiders after his July 11 trade to the Rangers organization. The Lone Star state was home to Betsy and Adrian from July to September. Adrian helped the RoughRiders get to the Texas League playoffs before they once again moved—this time to Peoria, Arizona, where he became a Peoria Saguaro during the Arizona Fall League. After three years of hard knocks in the minor leagues, Adrian had his chance to play major league baseball for the Texas Rangers in 2004.

The 2004 season for Adrian began with the Oklahoma Redhawks of Triple-A baseball in Oklahoma City. He played 123 games for the Redhawks, but 2004 was memorable because Gonzalez finally received his call to the major leagues when the Rangers first baseman, Mark Teixeira, suffered an injury. On April 18, Adrian joined the Rangers in Seattle, Washington, in a game against the Mariners. Adrian said of his first game, "I was taking infield and there was a pop fly down the line in right. I decided to see if I could get to it. What I didn't realize was that there was a screen down the line to protect fans from being hit during batting practice. I ran full speed into that screen. Never saw it."[19] Two days later versus the Anaheim Angels, Adrian got his first major league hit.

On April 25, Adrian hit his first major league home run, which came after teammates Laynce Nix and Rob Barajas had each hit a home run, making Adrian the first Ranger to earn his first home run in a back-to-back-to-back home run effort. Four days later, Teixeira returned from his injury and Adrian returned to the Redhawks. He would not play with the Rangers again until September 13. During his 2005 campaign, Adrian earned more time with the Rangers, including a spot on the opening day roster. He was the only rookie on the starting roster that day. In total, Adrian started in 39 games with the Rangers in 2005, but once again played the majority of the season with the Redhawks. After the season was over, Adrian and Betsy moved to Mazatlan to play winter baseball for the Mexican Pacific League. Adrian was a member of the Venados de Mazatlan; it would be the last minor league experience he would have as a member of the Texas Rangers organization.

In an interview with Bill Mitchell, Adrian expressed his enjoyment at being on the Mazatlan team, "I grew up with baseball out here. It's something that's different. In the States the fans cheer, but the name calling and cussing and all the things that go on here, you get to have fun with them [the fans]."[20] Adrian proved to be an asset to the American players playing in the league for the first time. According to Adrian, "I've been their 'go to' guy whenever they need a translation of where to go or if this food is okay to eat…the whole deal. I tell them the food is the same thing as over there…you'll only get sick if you think you're going to get sick."[21] Gonzalez's time in Mexico allowed fine-tuning to his hitting while working with veteran Mexican pitchers.

Prior to Christmas on December 20, 2005, Adrian received word that the Rangers had traded him along with pitcher Chris Young and outfielder Terrmel Sledge for pitchers Adam Eaton and Akinori Otsuka. Adrian told Bill Center, "It's like coming back to two homes. Even before the trade was completed, I was hearing from family and friends on both sides of the border."[22] Since Adrian and Betsy's marriage in 2003, the couple had moved twenty-four different times. Now they would settle in San Diego, where it all began. Before he joined the Padres, however, Adrian played for one more team. Adrian played as first baseman for Mexico's team in the first World Baseball Classic in late winter 2006. Adrian told *San Diego Union-Tribune* sports writer, Tom Krasovic, "I'm really anxious to get out there and defend my country."[23] Team Mexico won games against

Canada and South Africa to advance from the first round to
the second. Their only loss was against the United States team.
However, in round two, the Mexican team eliminated the
United States in a tight 2 - 1 ball game. In turn, losses to Korea
and Japan eliminated Mexico. With the World Baseball Classic
complete, Adrian joined his new team for spring training in
Peoria, Arizona.

Coming Full Circle

After the acquisition of Adrian by the Padres, Bill Center
noted, "The Padres hope Gonzalez will become a favorite with
a largely untapped—and potentially huge—segment of fans
straddling the border."[24] Earlier in his report Center mentioned,
"Tijuanans view Gonzalez as one of their own, a player who
spent his youth playing on the fields near the Tijuana airport—
one of which now bears his name."[25] There was much excitement
among Adrian's friends and family. He told an associated press
writer, "Friends and family have already bought 40 season
tickets, and there's probably a lot more that I haven't [thought]
of that are going to be there, so it'll be fun."[26] Even though
Adrian was on the roster, he still had to wait his turn. The
Padres already had a starting first baseman in Ryan Klesko from
Westminster, California. However, prior to the beginning of the
season, Klesko suffered a shoulder injury that allowed Adrian to
start the season at first base.

In 2006, Adrian shone on the field and was named the team's
most valuable player. Some of his statistical highlights include:

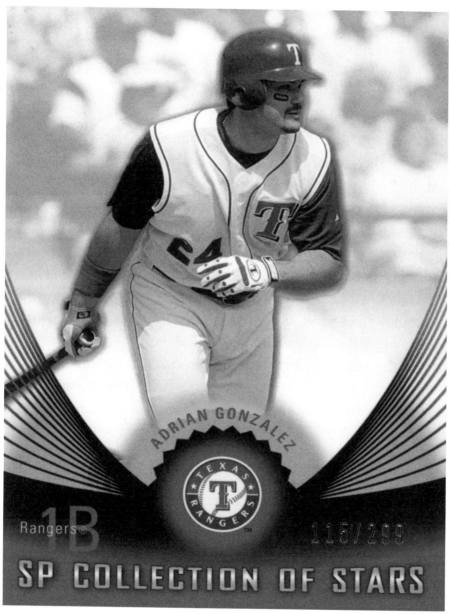

Adrian earns his chance to start in the Major Leagues while a member of the Texas Rangers, 2005. Author's Collection.

ending the season with a .304 batting average, hitting 38 doubles, 24 home runs, 82 RBIs, and earning 83 runs. He played in 156 games, which was the first time he had played more than 50 games in a major league season. From May 17 to June 19, Adrian had a 17-game hitting streak. In seven games from July 7 to 17, Gonzalez hit 7 home runs and was named the National League Player of the Week for July 17 to 23. More importantly, Adrian led the Padres to a NL Western Division title and the post season. Unfortunately, the Padres were swept by the St. Louis Cardinals.

Because of his efforts in 2006, Adrian was signed to a contract extension through 2010 prior to the 2007 season. Bill Center reported, "The Padres and Gonzalez, 25, yesterday announced a $9.5 million contract that runs through 2010 with the club holding an option for 2011 at $5.5 million."[27] Adrian said of the deal, "I didn't want to ever be in a situation where I was thinking about hitting a homer to help my numbers for arbitration when I should be moving a runner along. I want to play baseball that will help the Padres. I am happy the way this worked out."[28] Later, he told Center: "I want to stay here. This is the team I admired while growing up. But this is also a deal that secures life for Betsy and myself. Security was important to me."[29] Adrian looked for further security, but not of the financial kind in July 2007, when he received a death threat message on his cell phone.

While shopping with his wife at Ralph's grocery store on July 20, 2007, Adrian listened to his voice mail and to his horror heard a male voice stating, "We are going to kill you. Your father

Adrian and older brother Edgar discuss strategy during a game. Author's Collection.

is worthless."[30] According to Joe Hughes of the *San Diego Union-Tribune*, "His [Adrian's] father, David Gonzalez, was a majority owner of the Tijuana Potros professional baseball team and recently had a falling out with other partners, dissolving the partnership and selling the club."[31] Padres CEO Sandy Alderson said, "We are taking this very seriously. Law enforcement is involved."[32] The call was traced to Whittier, California. Irasema Mayoral Liera of the *San Diego Union-Tribune* investigated the

business dealing between David Gonzalez and his partner
Belisario Cabrera. According to Liera's report, "David Gonzalez,
who lives in Chula Vista, said he and a partner put down $1
million to buy the Tijuana Potros in December 2004. A few
months later their relationship soured over conflicts concerning
control of the team."[33] David Gonzalez sold his 65 percent of the
team to Cabrera, but never got paid. Cabrera's assets were frozen
after a total of fourteen lawsuits. David reclaimed control of the
team. However, he has avoided crossing the border since Adrian
received the death threat. He operates the team from his office in
the South Bay.

Only missing one game in 2007, Adrian played a total of 161
games for the Padres. He started out the season just as hot as
he ended 2006 by setting a new franchise record for most RBIs
in a month (25) and tying a monthly home run record (7). He
finished the season with 30 home runs and once again played a
major role in the Padres playoff push. Yet, facing the Colorado
Rockies in a one game playoff for the final wild card slot on
October 1, 2007, the Padres post season hopes were dashed in
an incredible 13 inning affair. Corey Brock of *mlb.com* illustrated
Adrian's contribution to the game, "Trailing, 3-0, San Diego
took a 5-3 lead when Adrian Gonzalez hit his 30th home run of
the season, a grand slam off Rockies starter Josh Fogg."[34] Scott
Hairston added to the Padres lead, breaking a tie in the top of
the 13th inning with a two run home run. The Padres were three
outs from going back to the playoffs for a third consecutive
season. According to Brock, "For the second time in three days,
Hoffman blew a save in a critical moment, though this time it

cost him much more than pride. It cost Hoffman and the Padres a chance to move on to the postseason for the third consecutive year."[35] The Padres lost the epic battle 9-8, and the Rockies went on to represent the National League in the World Series.

The 2008 Padre season ended with one loss short of 100 on the season. It was one of the organization's worst seasons in history. Adrian's performance, however, was one of the few positives for the team. He played in every game and ended the season with 172 hits, 119 RBIs, and 36 home runs. Beyond statistics, the season was enjoyable for Adrian because his brother Edgar was called up on May 12. It was Edgar's first appearance in the major leagues. Bill Center wrote, "It was hard to tell who was happier yesterday, Adrian Gonzalez or older brother Edgar, who joined the Padres in Wrigley Field after being promoted from Triple-A Portland."[36] In addition, "Alba and David Gonzalez flew in from San Diego to see their sons become the fourth set of brothers to play for the Padres at the same time."[37] Adrian told Center, "I'm extremely excited. It began to feel like it might never happen for Edgar and that wouldn't have been right. I don't think the game has been exactly fair to him."[38] In the game, Edgar got his first major league hit and RBI in the seventh inning. Adrian went 1-4, but the Padres lost 12-3. Despite the final score, the Gonzalez brothers were happy to be reunited and a part of the Padres' history. The other brother duos to take the field at the same time for the Padres were Marcus and Brian Giles in 2007, Tony and Chris Gwynn in 1996, and Roberto and Sandy Alomar 1988–89.

Along with the excitement of having Edgar join the Padres,

2008 was a rewarding year for Adrian and Betsy Gonzalez. They launched the Adrian & Betsy Gonzalez foundation on September 2, 2008, during a dinner benefit featuring Padres players playing cook and server to the guests in attendance. Nicole Reino reported, "Adrian was the honorary chef for the evening. Dressed in whites, he manned the stove and prepared more than 100 guests a five-course dinner."[39] Padres' pitcher Heath Bell assisted in the kitchen while third baseman Kevin Kouzmanoff took orders while pitcher Clay Hensley served as bartender.

The motto of the foundation is "empowering underprivileged youth through athletics, education and health." The goal, as Adrian told *San Diego Magazine,* is this: "The kids are able to learn about work ethic and teamwork. For me, growing up was about learning perseverance – to keep working hard. Education is an important foundation for allowing kids to grow and become professionals in any area of life. We provide books, scholarships – anything that helps kids get the education they need."[40] The commitment to the foundation comes from the Gonzalez's strong religious beliefs. Adrian illustrated, "Because of my faith in Christ I do not feel any pressure to perform because performance on the field is not my goal in life. I work as hard as I can work and try and have it translate to results, but it doesn't make or break me, so it takes away any kind of pressure. My walk with Christ is what is important to me."[41] Adrian's dedication to his foundation, his belief in Christ, the devotion to his family, and his dependability as a member of the San Diego Padres are the components that make up the man—Adrian Gonzalez.

The Padres 2009 season will be their fortieth season in San Diego. It will also be a challenging test for Adrian. Many will look upon him as a leader of the team along with outfielder Brian Giles, since short stop Khalil Greene and their all-time saves leader, Trevor Hoffman, will no longer be playing for the Padres. Also, with the impending departure of ace pitcher Jake Peavy, the Padre fans may very well call upon Adrian's leadership to bring hope to his home team. Along with Edgar, the Gonzalez brothers play for two nations and two ethnic groups, all of whom cheer and yearn for a more prosperous Padre season in 2009.

Adrian is still a young man with a lot of baseball years remaining, but after his career, he plans to go back to college and obtain his degree in mechanical engineering. Adrian Gonzalez is an encouraging role model for Mexican children both in the United States and Mexico—as well as an extraordinary example of a San Diego-produced athlete.

Endnotes

1. Bill Center, "Happy to be home – Former Eastlake star Adrian Gonzalez welcomes trade to Padres," *The San Diego Union-Tribune,* February 6, 2006.
2. "Little Padres Parks," www.padres.com (accessed on December 3, 2008).
3. Adrian Gonzalez, interviewed by author, San Diego, CA, December 2, 2008.
4. Kirk Kenney, "Yo, Adrian! Eastlake First Baseman Adrian Gonzalez May Just Hear His Name Called First By Florida In Tomorrow's Major League Draft," *The San Diego Union-Tribune,* June 4, 2000.
5. Gonzalez, interviewed by author.
6. Adrian Gonzalez, "Biography," www.agonzalez23.com (accessed on December 1, 2008).
7. Center, "Happy to be home."
8. Kenney, "Yo, Adrian!"
9. Tom Sheridan, "HR-happy Eastlake gets USDHS in final," *The San Diego Union-Tribune,* May 30, 1999.
10. Kenney, "Yo, Adrian!" Coach David Gonzalez of Eastlake High was a star baseball player for the University of San Diego Toreros.
11. Ibid.
12. Ibid.
13. Kirk Kenney, "Diamonds in rough? S.D. No. 1 – Gonzalez leads the county as Ground Zero of baseball draft," *The San Diego Union-Tribune,* June 6, 2000.
14. Ibid.

15. Ibid.

16. All of Adrian Gonzalez's baseball statistics noted in this text can be found via his biography on www.padres.com

17. Gonzalez, "Biography."

18. Ibid.

19. "The Questions with Adrian Gonzalez," *Sports Illustrated*, Vol. 107, Issue 12, September 24, 2007.

20. Bill Mitchell, "Winter League Experience a Plus for Prospects Gonzalez, Gonzalez and Duncan," www.minorleaguewatch.com, November 2005 (accessed on December 3, 2008).

21. Ibid.

22. Center, "Happy to be home."

23. Tom Krasovic, "Castilla, Gonzalez eager to represent Mexico," *The San Diego Union-Tribune*, February 20, 2006.

24. Center, "Happy to be home."

25. Ibid.

26. Associated Press, "Sore left shoulder could land Klesko on DL," www.espn.com, March 29, 2006 (accessed on December 3, 2008).

27. Bill Center, "Gonzalez gets $9.5 mil deal through 2010." *The San Diego Union-Tribune*, April 2, 2007.

28. Ibid.

29. Ibid.

30. Joe Hughes, "Gonzalez receives a death threat," *The San Diego Union-Tribune*, July 24, 2007.

31. Ibid.

32. Ibid.

33. Irasema Mayoral Liera, "Adrian Gonzalez's father battling his ex-partner for debt, Potros," *The San Diego-Union Tribune*, August 23, 2007.

34. Corey Brock, "Padres lose heartbreaker in 13th," www.mlb.com, October 2, 2007 (accessed December 5, 2008).

35. Ibid.

36. Bill Center, "Gonzalez welcomes his brother to the big leagues—finally," *The San Diego Union-Tribune*, May 13, 2008.

37. Ibid.

38. Ibid.

39. Nicole Reino, "Adrian Gonzalez launches Foundation during dinner," *La Jolla Light*, September 3, 2008.

40. Julia Beeson Polloreno, "The Munificent Seven," *San Diego Magazine*, Vol. 60, Number 14, December 2008.

41. Gonzalez, interviewed by author.

MICKEY WRIGHT

LADIES PROFESSIONAL GOLF ASSOCIATION

LPGA Champion, Mickey Wright. Courtesy of the San Diego Hall of Champions.

Chapter VI

A Legacy of Champions

Beyond the five athletes discussed, there are numerous minority athletes born and raised in San Diego whose accomplishments are noteworthy and in many cases resulted from the trail blazed by those to whom this project has been devoted. Outstanding female athletes have taken their place in San Diego's sports history. Maureen Connolly was the first female to dominate the world of tennis and Tiffany Chin served as a positive role model for the female Asian American figure skaters who followed her. Three other notable women born and raised in San Diego also found success in sports where women had not previously gained much respect or notoriety.

Known for having the one of the best swings in both the women's and men's games, Mary Kathryn Wright, or "Mickey" as she was better known, dominated the Ladies Professional Golf Association (LPGA) from 1956 through 1969. Wright was born in San Diego on February 14, 1935. When she ended her career, Mickey had won 82 LPGA tournaments, which ranks second all-time. She also earned the most money on the tour for four consecutive seasons, 1961 through 1964. Mickey continues to be the only player in LPGA history to hold all four major titles at the same time. *Golf Digest* voted Mickey the 9th greatest

Olympic star Gail Devers in action at the Olympic Games in Atlanta, Georgia, 1996. Courtesy of the San Diego Hall of Champions.

golfer in the history of the sport in 2000. Betsy Rawls wrote of Mickey's passion for the sport, "Of all the qualities that led to Mickey's success, her drive to be the best was the thing that fueled her career. Mickey had to win. She felt that a lessening of her obsession diminished her chances of winning. Mickey could never tolerate being anything but the best, and she knew herself well enough to know when the time came that being the best took more out of her than she had to offer."[1] On October 10, 2007, Mickey was diagnosed with breast cancer, but fortunately survived and continues to live in Port St. Lucie, Florida.

Gail Devers grew up in National City and graduated from Sweetwater High School. She is a three time Olympic gold medalist in track and field. In 1992 at the games in Barcelona, Spain, Devers brought home her first gold medal in the 100 meter race. She retained her title four years later in Atlanta, Georgia and added a gold in 4x100 meter relay. She holds the distinction of being one of San Diego's most decorated African American Olympians.

With the passage of Title IX by President Richard Nixon in 1972 that stated, "No person in the United States shall, on the basis of sex, be excluded from participation in, be denied the benefits of, or be subjected to discrimination under any program or activity receiving Federal financial assistance,"[2] Ann Meyers-Drysdale was the first woman to receive a four-year athletic scholarship when the University of California Los Angeles offered the prize to her in 1976. She was born in San Diego on March 26, 1955. Meyers became an imposing force on the UCLA women's basketball team. In 1976, along with Greg Louganis, Ann represented the United States at the summer Olympics in

Montreal, Canada. The United States women's basketball team
won the silver medal. In a historic first, the Indiana Pacers of
the National Basketball Association signed Ann to a contract in
1980. She did not make the cut, but was the first woman ever to
be signed by an NBA team. She was a pioneer in the creation
of first the Women's Professional Basketball League and later
the WNBA. She married Los Angeles Dodgers pitching great
Don Drysdale in 1986 only to become a widow seven years later
following Drysdale's untimely passing. Today she is president of
the WNBA's Phoenix Mercury and vice president of the NBA's
Phoenix Suns. Ann Meyers-Drysdale is undoubtedly an inspiration to women who not only want to play basketball, but who
strive for executive roles in the male-dominated sports profession.

The number of men from minority backgrounds honored for
their athletic endeavors has increased over the years. Charlie
Powell was one of two African Americans to start for the San
Francisco 49'ers in 1952. Since then, many African American
National Football League players have been products of San
Diego. Charlie's brother, Art Powell, was one of the most
dominant wide receivers during the 1960s. He played for the
Philadelphia Eagles, Minnesota Vikings, and Buffalo Bills, but
it was his years with the New York Titans, who later became
the Jets, and the Oakland Raiders in which Art Powell's athletic
abilities made him a star. His career with the Raiders began
a season after Charlie retired. On one occasion, Art, along
with several teammates, refused to play an exhibition game
because the seating within the stadium was segregated. He
remains eighteenth on the all-time touchdown receiving list.

Terrell Davis looks for a lane while playing in Super Bowl XXXII at Qualcomm Stadium in San Diego, California, 1998. Davis was named the game's MVP. Courtesy of the San Diego Hall of Champions.

Ricky Williams. Courtesy of the San Diego Hall of Champions.

Three remarkable NFL running backs were born in San Diego. Marcus Allen, born on March 26, 1960 in San Diego, attended Abraham Lincoln High and served as a role model for Terrell Davis and Ricky Williams. Allen, along with his Los Angeles Raiders team, won the Super Bowl in 1984. Allen was named the game's MVP. His career spanned from 1982 to 1997 when he retired as a Kansas City Chief. In 2003, Marcus Allen was named to the Professional Football Hall of Fame, the highest honor for any football player. Terrell Davis not only followed Allen's footsteps in becoming a Super Bowl MVP, 1998, he also graduated from the same high school. Ricky Williams continues to play for the Miami Dolphins. He was selected fifth overall in the 1999 NFL draft after winning the Heisman Trophy.

A discussion on San Diego produced football players cannot be complete without the mention of Junior Seau. Seau's status among San Diego's most popular athletes is unchallenged. He was born Tiaina Baul Seau, Jr. on January 19, 1969, in San Diego, grew up in Oceanside, and graduated from Oceanside High School. Junior played twelve seasons with the San Diego Chargers and each year was named to the All-Star team. In 1995, Seau helped the Chargers win the AFC Championship and earn a spot in the Super Bowl. The Chargers lost to the San Francisco 49'ers 49-26 and the team has not been back since. The Chargers traded Seau to the Miami Dolphins in 2003 where he played two seasons before ending his career with the New England Patriots. Along with Dan Marino and Tim Brown, Seau is noted as one of the greatest NFL players to have never won a Super Bowl. Since being traded from the Chargers, no one has yet to wear his num-

Tony Gwynn in mid-swing. Courtesy of the San Diego Hall of Champions.

ber 55 jersey. Junior Seau's restaurant in Mission Valley remains a popular location to eat and watch Chargers games, while the Junior Seau Foundation strives, "to educate and empower young people through the support of child abuse prevention, drug and alcohol awareness, recreational opportunities, anti-juvenile delinquency efforts and complimentary educational programs."[3] Even though Seau did not end his career playing for the Chargers, in the hearts and minds of San Diegans, he will always be one.[4]

Another icon may not have been born in San Diego, but his twenty years as a Padre earned him legendary status in San Diego. Tony Gwynn was born in Long Beach, California, and arrived in San Diego as a freshman at San Diego State University. Becoming an outstanding basketball as well as baseball star, he began his career with the Padres in 1981. From there he smashed the hitting records finishing his career with an impressive 3,141 hits. Along with the hits, Gwynn was named to the All-Star team 15 times; he won 5 gold gloves and 7 silver slugger awards. His number 19 has been retired by the Padres and the new ballpark in which the team plays, Petco Park, in San Diego's East Village, can be found at 19 Tony Gwynn Drive. Tony retired from the team in 2001 and went on to coach baseball at SDSU. Tony's son, Tony Jr. was added to the Padres roster prior to the 2009 season and wears number eighteen.

Two baseball players who were born in San Diego paved the way for Gwynn and other minority athletes. One of the most prolific hitters of all time, Ted Williams, who grew up a few streets away from Maureen Connolly, was of Mexican descent. His maternal grandparents, Pablo Venzor and Natalia Hernandez

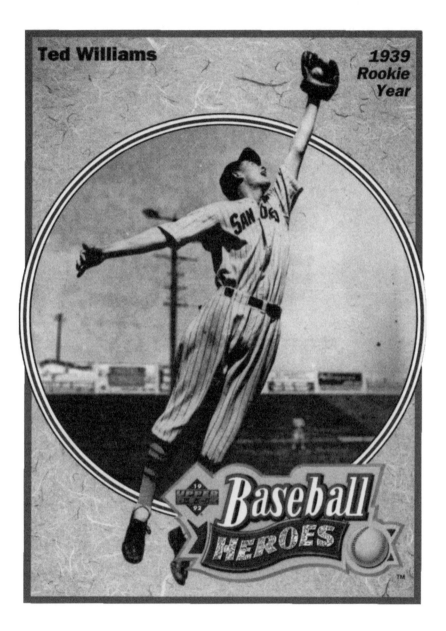

Ted Williams as a San Diego Padre, baseball card. Courtesy of the San Diego Hall of Champions.

were both born in Mexico. Ted Williams was born on August 30, 1918 and was given the name Theodore because of his father's admiration of Theodore Roosevelt. Williams played 19 major league seasons with the Boston Red Sox and if not for military service during World War II and Korea, might have set records in hitting statistics that could have been unattainable by any other player. He is still perceived to be the greatest hitter of all time.

John Ritchey was born in 1923 in San Diego and became known as "The Jackie Robinson of the Pacific Coast League." As Tom Shanahan wrote, "He broke the PCL color line in 1948 for the minor-league San Diego Padres at old Lane Field. It was a year after Ritchey, a catcher, was the Negro Leagues batting champion with a .381 average for the Chicago American Giants."[5] Ritchey, despite being an African American, earned home town hero status as a member of the Padres. However, as a teenager playing for

YESTERDAY'S BASEBALL

JOHN F. RITCHIE

John Ritchey as a San Diego Padre, baseball card. Courtesy of the San Diego Hall of Champions.

the American Legion Post No. 6, Ritchey dealt with segregation below the Mason-Dixon Line when he was barred from playing in the league's 1940 championship held in North Carolina. Despite the cruelties of Jim Crow, Ritchey's career with the San Diego Padres of the Pacific Coast League was impressive and led to desegregation throughout the rest of the league. The San Diego Padres honored Ritchey in 2008 with a sculpture at Petco Park. Dick Freeman, Padres President and CEO stated, "Johnny Ritchey is not only a Padres legend, he is an important part of the history of San Diego. As a member of the Padres, he paved the way for African Americans in the Pacific Coast League. We're proud to honor him with this special tribute."[6]

On May 29, 1989, Michael Chang became the first Chinese-American to win a Grand Slam tennis event when he defeated Stefan Edberg in an exciting five set match at the French Open. Chang was born in New Jersey, but moved to Encinitas, California where he attended San Dieguito High School until the 10th grade when he quit school to focus solely on his tennis career. Chang's father was born on mainland China, but like Tiffany Chin's father, escaped to Taiwan after the communist revolution. The French Open was Chang's only major title, yet it was an extraordinary first for an Asian athlete in a white dominated sport. Billie Jean King stated, "Michael Chang was and still is a big thing in Asia. He was the first Asian to get global sponsorship that provided him with exposure and recognition in the country and especially Asia. He also has the perfect personality to connect with the Asian population. That is why he is a champion." [7]

A young Michael Chang competes. Courtesy of the San Diego Hall of Champions.

Endnotes

1. Guy Yocom, "50 Greatest Golfers of All-Time and what they taught us," *Golf Digest*, July 2000.
2. http://www.ed.gov/about/offices/list/ocr/docs/tix_dis.html accessed December 1, 2008.
3. Junior Seau quote accessed from http://www.juniorseau.org/ on December 1, 2008.
4. On December 5, 2008, Junior Seau re-signed with the New England Patriots. Seau said, "What it took was a coach that you respect made a call, come out and help guys that you have a lot of love for. Obviously, there's a lot of history here with us and it wasn't a hard decision. You just care for the guys in this locker room and you care for the coach and organization and that's the only reason I'm here."
5. Tom Shanahan, "Johnny Ritchey's Silent Protest," *voicesofsandiego. org*, June 17, 2008.
6. "Padres honor Johnny Ritchey with sculpture at PETCO Park," *padres.com*, March 30, 2005.
7. Billie Jean King, interviewed by author, Newport Beach, CA, October 10, 2007.

Afterword

Whereas San Diego's professional sports franchises, past and present, have unfortunately been under the spell of what has been popularly called the "San Diego Sports Curse,"[1] the county has managed to produce a number of exceptional athletes in all areas of sport. These athletes have won numerous championships, broken down racial barriers, reached the pinnacle of their individual sport, and brought acclaim and praise to San Diego. This book has explored the lives of five complex individuals who overcame personal and physical odds to achieve their athletic goals. Whether they were struck down too early, had their bodies give out on them, simply chose to end their careers on their own terms, or are still competing in the hopes of bringing a World Series championship to San Diego, each of the athletes detailed represent a San Diego where no matter an individual's race, color, creed, gender, or sexual orientation, dreams of athletic accomplishment can be achieved. They are the examples of how it can be done.

There may not be a World Series trophy on display at Petco Park or a Super Bowl championship banner hanging at Qualcomm Stadium, but San Diego certainly has produced champions of every variety and from multiple sports. It is important to note that without the acceptance of these great athletes for who they were/are, San Diego may never have had the opportunity

to see who they became and revel in the accomplishments they
achieved for themselves and for San Diego. With the racial and
sexual barriers continuing to come down, there will be a time, it
is hoped, when athletes are no longer seen as minority athletes,
but simply athletes.

Endnotes

1. The San Diego Sports Curse is a superstition believed by San
    Diegans based on the fact that no major sports franchise playing
    in San Diego has ever won its championship. The Chargers
    have played for 38 years in San Diego. They won the AFL
    Championship their first and only season in Los Angeles. The
    Padres have been a member of Major League Baseball for 40 years
    and have yet to win a World Series. San Diego had two NBA
    teams, the Clippers for 6 seasons and the Rockets for 4 seasons.
    Neither team won the NBA championship while in San Diego.
    Finally, none of these teams has an overall winning record during
    their combined seasons in San Diego. For more information on
    the curse, see Mark Zeigler's article, "San Diego is No. 1 in a lot of
    things, but in major pro team sports, it's still the biggest city that
    hasn't won the Big Trophy. No Super Bowl, no World Series (and
    no chance in the NBA or NHL)," *San Diego Union-Tribune*, February
    11, 2007.

Bibliography

Newspapers

"Chin Enjoys Status of Being 'Special'," *The San Diego Union*, December 14, 1980.

"Ex-49er Powell Quits Ring For Bid with Raiders," *Los Angeles Times*, July 13, 1960.

"Funeral Rites Salute 'Little Mo,'" *San Diego Union*, May 22, 1969.

"Holiday on Ice signs Chin to 2-year, $1 million pact." *The San Diego Union*, October 3, 1987.

"Little Mo Goes to College," *San Diego Union*, May 28, 1964.

"Louganis 'Fears' Manager he Fired," *San Diego Tribune*, March 29, 1989.

"Prep Sports Roundup." *San Diego Union*, May 4, 1977.

"San Diego's Tiffany Chin Wins World Skating Title," *The San Diego Union*, December 14, 1980.

Bell, Norman, "Li'l Mo Wins Third Female Athlete of the Year, Flo 2nd Again," *San Diego Union*, January 9, 1954.

Beyette, Beverly, "The Legend of 'Little Mo'," *Los Angeles Times*, September 5, 1978.

Bisheff, Steve, "Louganis Tells why he Almost Became Diving Dropout," *San Diego Evening Tribune*, April 20, 1977.

Brooks, Joe, "Little Mo's Tennis Game was Simply Devastating," *San Diego Union*, June 13, 1974.

Canepa, Nick, "Tiffany Chin: From Mira Mesa to the upper echelon," *San Diego Tribune*, February 4, 1984.

Center, Bill, "Gonzalez gets $9.5 mil deal through 2010." *The San Diego Union-Tribune*, April 2, 2007.

_____ "Gonzalez welcomes his brother to the big leagues – finally," *The San Diego Union-Tribune*, May 13, 2008.

_____ "Happy to be home – Former Eastlake star Adrian Gonzalez welcomes trade to Padres," *The San Diego Union-Tribune*, February 6, 2006.

Cleeland, Nancy, "At age 13, Tiffany Chin already had shown she's more than just a good skate," *San Diego Evening Tribune*, December 10, 1980.

Coat, Tom, "A turning point for Trenary," *San Diego Tribune*, February 9, 1987.

_____ "Chin beckons, and the world comes running," *San Diego Tribune*, February 27, 1984.

_____ "Greg Louganis Already A Part of Diving's Greatest Scenes, He Continues to Make a Splash and Spread the Word," *San Diego Union*, May 21, 1985.

_____ "She's Growing up, so are the Skates," *San Diego Tribune*, February 14, 1983.

_____ "The demands build on Chin," *San Diego Tribune*, January 26, 1985.

Connolly, Will, "Charlie Powell Sweats Off the Grid Blubber," *Los Angeles Times*, March 21, 1954.

Crowe, Jerry, "Comeback at Tiffany's," *Los Angeles Times*, February 1, 1987.

Daley, Arthur, "Election of Professions," *Los Angeles Times*, 1956.

Davis, George T., "Albert Predicts Rosy Future for Powell in Fight Game," *Los Angeles Herald-Express*, June 19, 1954.

_____ "Powell's Return to Ring Compares Football, Boxing," *Los Angeles Herald-Express*, January 18, 1956.

Denny, Dick, "Chin 5th in Skating Finals," *The San Diego Union*, February 3, 1982.

Downey, Mike, "Louganis Makes it Look Easy," *Los Angeles Times*, August 20, 1988.

Esper, Dwain, "Ex-Grid Star Earns Big Time Bout With 6 Round TKO Victory," *Hayward Daily Review*, September 3, 1954.

Fisher, Nelson, "Maureen Connolly Injured on Horse," *The San Diego Union*, July 21, 1954.

Fiske, Jack, "Powell KO's Jones 50 Seconds of First," *San Francisco Chronicle*, July 14, 1954.

Gallup, Dave, "Tennis Great 'Mo' Connolly Dies in Dallas," *San Diego Union*, May 22, 1969.

Hagen, Howard, "Powell Kayoes Foe In Second, Runs Skein to 8," *The San Diego Union*, June 26, 1954.

Hall, John, "Boxing First Powell Dream," *Los Angeles Mirror*, May 16, 1954.

Harvey, Randy, "On the Chin," *Los Angeles Times*, January 25, 1988.

Hawn, Jack, "World of Charlie Powell," *Los Angeles Times*, January 23, 1963.

Hersh, Phil, "Chin's question: Time not Talent," *Independent Press Service*, March 1, 1984.

Hoffer, Richard, "The Comeback of Tiffany Chin," *Los Angeles Times*, December 14, 1985.

Hughes, Joe, "Gonzalez receives a death threat," *The San Diego Union-Tribune*, July 24, 2007.

Jenkins, Chris, "Chin Up, She Says," *The San Diego Union*, February 4, 1987.

_____ "Chin upstages ice queens, finishes 2nd," *The San Diego Union*, January 22, 1984.

_____ "Cold blood comes hard to Tiffany," *The San Diego Union*, January 1, 1984.

_____ "Louganis Perched Alone at the Top," *The Orange County Register*, August 8, 1984.

_____ "Louganis still Breaking Barriers," *The Orange County Register*, July 24, 1985.

_____ "Powell hit with Power in Three Sports," *San Diego Union*, February 14, 1995.

Kay, Linda, "Louganis Stays Light on his Feet with Life of Dancing and Diving," *San Diego Union*, February 2, 1978.

Kenney, Kirk, "Diamonds in rough? S.D. No. 1 – Gonzalez leads the county as Ground Zero of baseball draft," *The San Diego Union-Tribune*, June 6, 2000.

_____ "Yo, Adrian! Eastlake First Baseman Adrian Gonzalez May Just Hear His Name Called First By Florida In Tomorrow's Major League Draft," *The San Diego Union-Tribune*, June 4, 2000.

Krasovic, Tom, "Castilla, Gonzalez eager to represent Mexico," *The San Diego Union-Tribune*, February 20, 2006.

Liera, Irasema Mayoral, "Adrian Gonzalez's father battling his ex-partner for debt, Potros," *The San Diego-Union Tribune*, August 23, 2007.

Magee, Jerry, "Connolly's feel for the game made her huge on the tennis court." *San Diego Union-Tribune*, December 21, 1999.

McDonald, Johnny, "Powell Flattens Jones in Second," *San Diego Union*, December 6, 1958.

Mossman, John, "Chin skating on a thin edge at national finals," *San Diego Tribune*, February 3, 1986.

Muller, Eddie, "Too Much Praise for Charley Powell Can Cause Him Harm at This Time," *San Francisco Examiner*, July 14, 1954.

Murphy, Jack, "Loss To Norkus Haunts Powell As He Tries Boxing Comeback," *San Diego Union*, December 4, 1958.

_____ "Maureen Annexes 3rd Wimbledon Net Crown," *San Diego Union*, July 4, 1954.

_____ "Powell Appears Overmatched But He Doesn't Think So," *San Diego Union*, March 4, 1959.

_____ "Powell's Astonishing Triumph Opens up a Bright Ring Future," *San Diego Union*, March 5, 1959.

Ortman, Bob, "Powell Faces Buford In Debut Here Tonight," *San Diego Union*, May 28, 1954.

Ostler, Scott, "Louganis Answers Olympic Pressure With a Perfect Dive," *Los Angeles Times*, September 27, 1988.

Petix, Steve, "San Diego to host U.S. skating event," *The Daily Californian*, January 31, 1981.

Pye, Jr., Brad, "Why Did Powell Quit Football," *Santa Cruz Sentinel*, August 2, 1955.

Reilly, Rick, "To Louganis, Diving's the Easiest Part," *Los Angeles Times*, January 10, 1984.

Reino, Nicole, "Adrian Gonzalez launches Foundation during dinner," *La Jolla Light*, September 3, 2008.

Savage, Jeff, "Louganis not Afraid to Flop," *San Diego Union*, August 8, 1988.

Sheridan, Tom, "HR-happy Eastlake gets USDHS in final," *The San Diego Union-Tribune*, May 30, 1999.

Smith, Liz, "Plunging Into N.Y. Theater," *Los Angeles Times*, August 17, 1983.

Spielvogel, Jill, "A Top Competitor Steps Aside for his Dogs," *San Diego Union-Tribune*, August 26, 2002.

Voss, Arthur, "Give 'Em Hell, Mo!" *San Diego Union*, November 10, 1988.

Ward, Alan, "On Second Thought," *Oakland Tribune*, September 7, 1954.

White, Allen, "Reagan's AIDS Legacy Silence Equals Death," *San Francisco Gate*, June 8, 2004.

Wilbon, Michael, "A Platform of Grace and Courage," *Washington Post*, March 6, 1995.

Zimmerman, Paul, "Sportscripts," *Los Angeles Times*, July 13, 1954.

Books

Brinker-Simmons, Cindy, *Little Mo's Legacy: A Mother's Lessons. A Daughter's Story*. Irving, Texas: Tapestry Press, 2001.

Buck, Ray, *Tiffany Chin: A Dream on Ice*. Chicago: Childrens Press, 1986.
Connolly, Maureen, *Forehand Drive*. London: MacGibbon and Kee, 1957.
Edwards, Roy, This is Maureen...*Tournament Program for Maureen Connolly Brinker Mixed Doubles Charity Tournament at the Dallas Country Club*. Media Guide. May 24–25, 1968.
Jordan, Pat, *The Best Sports Writings of Pat Jordan*. New York: Persea Books, 2008.
Louganis, Greg and Eric Marcus, *Breaking the Surface*. New York: Random House, 1995.
Wiggins, David K. and Patrick B. Miller, *The Unlevel Playing Field*. Chicago, University of Illinois Press, 2003.
Zirin, Dave, *What's My Name, Fool: Sports and Resistance in the United States*. Chicago: Haymarket Books, 2005.

Personal Interviews

Adrian Gonzalez, interviewed by author, San Diego, CA, December 2, 2008.
Billie Jean King, interviewed by author, Newport Beach, CA, October 23, 2008.
Greg Louganis, interviewed by author, San Diego, CA, September 11, 2008.

Magazines

"The Questions with Adrian Gonzalez," *Sports Illustrated*, Vol. 107, September 24, 2007.
"Young Queen," *Time Magazine*, Vol. LVIII, September 17, 1951.
Grant, Reginald, "Mr. Versatility" – The Youngest Player in NFL History," *Black Sports The Magazine*, February 2006.
Greenspan, Bud, "The Highs, The Lows of Greg Louganis," *Parade Magazine*, September 11, 1988.
Morrison, Alec, "The Magnificent Little Mo," *Sports Illustrated*, August 27, 2001.
Olsen, Jack "Hysteria Is A Sometime Thing," *Sports Illustrated*, Vol. 24, April 25, 1966.
Ottum, Bob, "Guaranteed to Keep the Chin Up," *Sports Illustrated*, Vol. 62, February 4, 1985.

Polloreno, Julia Beeson, "The Munificent Seven," *San Diego Magazine*, Vol. 60, December 2008.

Swift, E.M., "A Message Worth Repeating," *Sports Illustrated*, Vol. 82, March 6, 1995.

_____ "Books or Blades, There's No Doubting Thomas," *Sports Illustrated*, Vol. 64, February 17, 1986.

Verschoth, Anita, "Winging on Toward Immortality," *Sports Illustrated*, Vol. 54, Issue 72.

Yocom, Guy, "50 Greatest Golfers of All-Time and what they taught us," *Golf Digest*, July 2000.

Internet Sources

"Castro: Profile of the great survivor." http://news.bbc.com.uk

"Little Padres Parks," www.padres.com

"Padres honor Johnny Ritchey with sculpture at PETCO Park," www.padres.com

"Sore left shoulder could land Klesko on DL," www.espn.com

Brock, Corey, "Padres lose heartbreaker in 13th," www.mlb.com

Elfman, Lois, "Behind the scenes of figure skating: Tiffany Chin's love of skating continues," www.icenetwork.com

Flatter, Ron, "Louganis Never Lost Drive to Dive," ESPN Sports Century Biography, 2007. This article can be accessed via http://espn.go.com/classic/biography/s/Louganis_Greg.html

Gonzalez, Adrian, "Biography," www.agonzalez23.com

http://en.wikipedia.org/wiki/Associated_Press_Athlete_of_the_Year

http://www.ed.gov/about/offices/list/ocr/docs/tix_dis.html

http://www.juniorseau.org/

Maureen Connolly Brinker Tennis Foundation, http://www.mcbtennis.org

Mitchell, Bill, "Winter League Experience a Plus for Prospects Gonzalez, Gonzalez and Duncan," www.minorleaguewatch.com

Scheurer, Ronald A., "Breaking the Ice: The Mabel Fairbanks story." http://findarticles.com/p/articles/mi_m1546/is_n6_v12/ai_20084308/pg_1

Shanahan, Tom, "Johnny Ritchey's Silent Protest," www.voicesofsandiego.org

Tiffany Chin interview with John Tesh prior to the 1986 world championships in Geneva, Switzerland, http://www.youtube.com/watch?v=m5W5EQqXBMU

Weisman, Jon, "A New Era Dawns: Tensions Mounted for Robinson on First
      Day," www.si.com, April 13, 2007.

Sunbelt Publications

Incorporated in 1988 with roots in publishing since 1973, Sunbelt produces and distributes natural science and outdoor guidebooks, regional histories and reference books, plus pictorials and stories that celebrate the land and its people. Our publishing program focuses on the Californias, which are today three states in two nations sharing one Pacific shore. Sunbelt books help to discover and conserve the natural history and cultural heritage of unique regions on the frontiers of adventure and learning. Our books guide readers into distinctive communities and special places, both natural and man-made.

We carry hundreds of books on San Diego and southern California!
Visit us online at:
www.sunbeltbooks.com